W9-ASY-411

CITIZENSHIP

WHAT EVERYONE NEEDS TO KNOW®

CITIZENSHIP

WHAT EVERYONE NEEDS TO KNOW®

PETER J. SPIRO

OXFORD
UNIVERSITY PRESS

Oxford University Press is a department of the University of Oxford. It furthers
the University's objective of excellence in research, scholarship, and education
by publishing worldwide. Oxford is a registered trade mark of Oxford University
Press in the UK and certain other countries.

"What Everyone Needs to Know" is a registered trademark of
Oxford University Press.

Published in the United States of America by Oxford University Press
198 Madison Avenue, New York, NY 10016, United States of America.

© Oxford University Press 2020

CIP data is on file at the Library of Congress
ISBN 978–0–19–091729–6 (pbk.)
ISBN 978–0–19–091730–2 (hbk.)

1 3 5 7 9 8 6 4 2

Paperback printed by LSC Communications, United States of America
Hardback printed by Bridgeport National Bindery, Inc., United States of America

To the memory of
my father, Herbert J. Spiro,
and grandfather, Howard C. Petersen.
Citizens both.

CONTENTS

2 Naturalization   25

3 Rights and Obligations of Citizenship   61

CITIZENSHIP

WHAT EVERYONE NEEDS TO KNOW®

INTRODUCTION

Citizenship is a like the air we breathe; it's all around us but often goes unnoticed. That is not a historically ordinary situation. Citizenship was once an exceptional status, a kind of aristocracy of the ancient world in which freedom and political voice were not taken for granted. Even as the nation-state emerged as the primary form of human association, citizenship remained an anomalous status, reserved for the few who were privileged as such in republican democracies. More recently, it has been the individual marker of membership in all national communities. It is generic; almost everyone has it, hence the ubiquity that has made it sometimes unseen. Most people never change the citizenship that they are unthinkingly born into; they have no cause to consider it any more critically than their choice of parents. Insofar as citizenship during the twentieth century came to be aligned with national community on the ground and in the public imagination, there was even less reason to look at it searchingly.

To the extent that it took residence in the public consciousness, "citizenship" came to represent an anodyne synonym for virtuousness in society and in individuals. It became the form of political address, a way of describing any public audience. Citizenship is something that everyone could agree on. It has consensus status across political divides. Citizenship telegraphs the shared equality among individuals

Citizenship. Peter J. Spiro, Oxford University Press (2020). © Oxford University Press.
10.1093/actrade/9780190917302.001.0001

in contemporary society, a status that anchors rights and individual dignity, something that frames the individual's place in the community. In the public imagination, citizenship has been considered an unalloyed good.

But citizenship is ripe for closer examination. Globalization, increased mobility, and growing anti-immigration politics highlight the fact that although most people in the world have citizenship someplace, there are vastly unequal entitlements attached to citizenship in particular countries. The universalized sense in which the word is used in political discourse in the United States masks the obvious fact that not everyone has US citizenship and that most of the world is excluded from it. To the extent an implication of equality holds fast within the citizenry, it clearly does not apply to those outside the fold. In more sedentary, state-oriented times, it was easy to blinder out those who were excluded from the citizenry because their citizenship was held in other, distinct communities largely out of view. Those communities were different enough that one could keep them at arm's length, a part of the natural order of things. The result has been a global kind of separate but equal.

That mindset is more difficult to sustain as national identities blur and distances are eclipsed. Citizenship still has its virtues. But as it more obviously marks the boundary of human community, citizenship is a tool of exclusion as well as inclusion. Citizenship has been a badge of equality. It may be turning into a badge of privilege. As citizenship is increasingly situated in a global context in which some have a "good" one and some do not, it is important to explore its meanings and mechanics.

This book addresses citizenship not as an institution to be venerated but as one that is contingent and constructed as a marker of membership in a state-based association. The book lays out the status fundamentals of citizenship: how one gets it, at birth and afterward through naturalization; how one loses it; what it gets you and what it demands of you by way of rights and obligations; how the once-reviled status of dual citizenship became broadly accepted; and how local and global citizenships along with nonstate memberships may complement or even displace national citizenship. This material is not offered as a practical guide, but rather as a lens on the past and future of citizenship and ultimately on the state itself. For example, territorial birthright citizenship is contested in the United States in the context of undocumented immigration, but the debate rarely stops to ask why location at moment of birth should determine one's citizenship and what that says about the demarcation of the national community. How can we justify making equality contingent on passing a test, as we do with naturalization applicants? What does the fact that some countries sell citizenship say about it as an institution? How has citizenship become cheap in the sense of requiring no distinctive obligations? How does dual citizenship undermine citizenship solidarities? In what circumstances should states be able to strip individuals of citizenship against their will? What are the implications of citizenries that no longer reflect social solidarities on the ground? These are the kinds of questions that start with the legal parameters of citizenship and lead to explorations of citizenship's broader significance in global society.

Citizenship has been a central organizing principle of modern global society and a primary dimension of individual identity. It may stay that way, but its ascendancy is being tested. As with any new challenge to an established institution, it is important to have some understanding of the backstory and how that backstory has shaped the current landscape. I hope this book will help orient critical thinking on a subject by those (most of us) who have not really thought about it at all.

A word on terminology and coverage: Today, "citizenship" and "nationality" are almost entirely synonymous. As a universal descriptor, however, "citizenship" is relatively new, accompanying the rise of constitutional democracy. Although not all countries are democratic, all countries now denominate their members as citizens. In the past, however, citizenship was a distinctive feature of democracy. Individuals belonging to other sovereignties were often called "subjects" for domestic purposes. As a matter of international law, "nationality" has historically been the term of art. For purposes of this book, then, historical discussions use "nationality," especially when describing developments beyond the United States (where "citizen" has been used from its founding).

The book also uses immigration-related terms that are necessarily incidental to citizenship status. "Permanent residence" indicates the status under which individuals are admitted to a country with no temporal limitations, a status available in almost all countries but which is extended under various labels. (In the United States, it is colloquially known as "green card" status after the color of the card that once evidenced the status.) "Non-immigrants" are those who are legally admitted but with limitations on activity (employment for instance), and usually also time. I use "unauthorized immigrant" to describe those who are present in the territory of a state in violation of immigration controls. Citizenship implicates full membership in a national community; it is distinct from immigration, which is about the regulation of entry into territory. But because access to territory comes with citizenship, and because immigration is often a predicate to citizenship, the two are inevitably coupled in some respects.

This book is about citizenship as a global institution and includes material from all global regions. It is more focused on citizenship practices in the Global North, to the extent that citizenship is largely an artifact of the West. That is certainly true as a historical matter. Nationality was once a matter deeply contested between European sovereigns and the United States in particular, and so the historical background, important to understanding citizenship's trajectory, is the history of nationality in those countries. Today, citizenship in developed economies remains more highly prized, precisely because of global inequalities, which translates into a focus on citizenship practices in those countries. There have nonetheless been interesting and consequential developments in citizenship practices among states of the Global South, which are also recounted in the pages that follow.

1

CITIZENSHIP THROUGH BIRTH

Why do states give anyone citizenship at birth?

As in all forms of human association, states are composed of individual members. In theory, states could delay the conferral of citizenship until individuals reach adulthood and the fully formed identity that comes with it. In practice, all states provide for citizenship at birth, and that is how the vast majority of the world's inhabitants acquire citizenship. From the state's perspective, birth citizenship is a practical necessity and an easy mechanism for replicating membership on an intergenerational basis.

There are two primary forms of birth citizenship: on the basis of place of birth and on the basis of parentage. Historically, these two forms of birth citizenship have been known as *jus soli*, which translates from Latin as "right of the soil," and *jus sanguinis*, or "right of the blood." The first is based on territorial location at time of birth, the second on parentage and ancestry. In some contexts, as discussed later in this chapter, they act in combination. Both imply a logic under which birth parameters predict a life trajectory. Birth citizenship is best justified on the grounds that circumstances surrounding birth—location, parentage, or both—point to subsequent membership in the national community.

Citizenship. Peter J. Spiro, Oxford University Press (2020). © Oxford University Press.
10.1093/actrade/9780190917302.001.0001

Does being born in a country's territory entitle
one to citizenship in that country?

In many countries, birth within national boundaries can lead to a grant of citizenship. In some, birth in a country's territory will automatically result in citizenship. The United States most famously practices this near-absolute form of birth citizenship. With the minor exception of the children born to diplomats, all persons born on US territory are US citizens at birth. This approach is common among Western Hemisphere states, including Canada, Mexico, and most Latin American countries.

Other countries have adopted modified *jus soli* birth citizenship mechanisms. Some states make automatic territorial birth citizenship contingent on parental immigration status. Children born on national territory to parents who are citizens will always have citizenship in that country. The United Kingdom, for example, extends citizenship to those born on UK soil to a permanent resident parent. Germany grants citizenship to individuals born on German territory if their noncitizen immigrant parents have resided in Germany for at least eight years prior to the birth of the child. Some European states, for example, Belgium, France, the Netherlands, and Portugal, restrict territorial birth citizenship to the children of parents who themselves were born on state territory. This is known as "double *jus soli*."

Some states will in certain cases require a combination of birth and subsequent residence on the part of the individual claiming citizenship. In the United Kingdom, a child born to temporary or unauthorized immigrant parents will not have automatic citizenship at birth. However, if that child remains habitually resident in the United Kingdom from birth until her tenth birthday, she is entitled to citizenship at that time. In Germany, eight years of noncitizen parental residence is a necessary but not sufficient condition for *jus soli*; on top of this the child must reside in Germany for eight years before she turns twenty-one, failing which birth citizenship will expire.

The global trend is to allow birth citizenship based on place of birth in at least some circumstances. Most states, for instance, extend citizenship at birth to those born on state territory of unknown parentage (so-called foundlings), to reduce the incidence of statelessness. More important, an increasing number of countries now recognize at least double *jus soli* birth citizenship; in other words, more states now confer citizenship on intergenerational immigrants than was historically the case.

But many countries continue to reject *jus soli* citizenship in all cases except when statelessness would result, including Austria, Finland, Indonesia, Egypt, Botswana, Kenya, and most Middle Eastern states. Some even fail to extend citizenship when statelessness will be the consequence, as is the case in India, Thailand, Nigeria, and Zambia. In these countries it is possible to have noncitizenship status persist on an indefinite, intergenerational basis. For example, a person born in one of these countries to parents and grandparents who were also born in that country but lack citizenship will not have citizenship at birth. Even when it doesn't increase the risk of statelessness, this older model poses human rights concerns, to the extent that lack of citizenship results in status inequality. For example, without territorial birth citizenship a fourth-generation legal resident would still lack full political rights.

What are the origins of territorial birthright citizenship?

Absolute territorial birthright citizenship has its roots in the feudal era. Under medieval conceptions of natural order, individuals were born into the protection of sovereigns, to whom they owed perpetual allegiance in return. Automatically and for life, they were subjects of the sovereign in whose territory they were born. The principle was notably articulated in the 1608 decision by the English Court of the King's Bench in *Calvin's Case*, which considered whether a person born in Scotland after James I's ascension to the English crown qualified as an English subject. As recounted by Sir Edward Coke, one of fourteen judges sitting on the case, "Every one born within the dominions of the King of England . . . is subject to all the duties and entitled to all the rights and liberties of an Englishman." It was by virtue of this common law interpretation (there was no statute governing the issue) that persons born in the American colonies were considered British subjects.

How does territorial birth citizenship relate to the Dred Scott decision?

The US Supreme Court's 1857 decision in the *Dred Scott* case addressed the question of whether free blacks were capable of holding US citizenship. At the time of its adoption in 1789, the US Constitution failed to address birth citizenship. Through the common law practice inherited from the United Kingdom, white persons born on US territory were assumed to have US citizenship at birth. In *Dred Scott*, the Supreme Court ruled that persons of African descent could not hold national citizenship even if they were free. (The heart of the dispute was whether a slave owner's move to a non-slave territory had resulted in Scott's emancipation, but the Court had to consider the citizenship issue since only citizens could invoke the Court's jurisdiction.)

The Court turgidly and illogically argued that various disabilities suffered by blacks evidenced that the Constitution's drafters could not have contemplated African American citizenship. The decision was better explained by the constitutional mechanics of citizenship, under which each state would have to respect the "privileges and immunities" of US citizens present in other states. If free blacks could hold citizenship, they would be entitled to travel freely in slaveholding states, a prospect in which slaveholding interests saw an intolerable threat. That explains why the question of black citizenship had been left open in the Constitution itself; abolitionist interests would have rejected a bar on blacks holding citizenship, while the slaveholding states would never have accepted black citizenship. *Dred Scott* forced the question and accelerated the road to civil war.

In 1868 the Constitution was amended to resolve the issue of black citizenship definitively. The Fourteenth Amendment provides that "all persons born in the United States, and subject to the jurisdiction thereof, are citizens of the United States and of the State wherein they reside."

Do all persons born in US territory enjoy US citizenship under the Fourteenth Amendment?

While the Fourteenth Amendment extended birth citizenship to blacks born in US states, its application to other groups was unclear. In its 1884 decision in *Elk v. Wilkins,* the Supreme Court found that Native Americans born into tribal membership were not "subject to the jurisdiction" of the United States and thus ineligible for citizenship at birth. Native Americans were extended birth citizenship by statute under the Indian Citizenship Act of 1924, which remains in effect today.

The Fourteenth Amendment's coverage was also contested with respect to the children of noncitizens born in the United States. In its 1898 decision in *Wong Kim Ark,* the Supreme Court considered the citizenship of a person born in San Francisco to legal immigrants from China. The immigrant parents were themselves barred from citizenship under then-applicable laws disqualifying Asians from naturalization. Nonetheless, the Court found the children of such immigrants entitled to birth citizenship under the Fourteenth Amendment. The Court concluded that the Fourteenth Amendment codified the *jus soli* birth citizenship rule inherited from British rule and the common law. The Court did not act out of any concern for the children of Chinese immigrants. Rather, the Court understood that birthright citizenship was key to the American experience. "To hold that the Fourteenth Amendment of the Constitution excludes from citizenship the children, born in the United States, of citizens or subjects of other countries," the

Court observed, "would be to deny citizenship to thousands of persons of English, Scotch, Irish, German, or other European parentage who have always been considered and treated as citizens of the United States." The *Wong Kim Ark* decision established an expansive rule of territorial birth citizenship in the United States.

What are the arguments for and against birthright citizenship for unauthorized immigrants?

As a matter of long-standing administrative practice and consistent with *Wong Kim Ark*, US citizenship has been extended to children born in the United States to unauthorized immigrant parents. In 2014 an estimated 275,000 children, or 7 percent of all births in the United States, had at least one unauthorized immigrant parent. The practice has long been politically contested. It is the most notable context in which anti-immigration constituencies have targeted a citizenship rule.

In their 1985 book *Citizenship Without Consent*, respected scholars Peter Schuck and Rogers Smith challenged the constitutional assumption that the Fourteenth Amendment mandates birth citizenship for the children of unauthorized immigrants. The authors highlighted the constitutional purpose of the American founders to abandon the ascriptive practice of feudal England in favor of a consent-based system of political membership. Since unauthorized immigrants by definition lack consent for their presence, their children should not enjoy any citizenship entitlement. Schuck and Smith also argued that the Fourteenth Amendment could not have covered birth citizenship for the children of unauthorized immigrants given the absence of federal immigration controls at the time of its adoption; there were no unauthorized immigrants at that time. Finally, the book highlighted the additional incentive that birth citizenship creates for unauthorized immigration. Would-be mothers who understand that a child born in the United States will automatically have birth citizenship, they argued, will have all the more reason to enter illegally.

There are strong arguments in favor of the established practice. The existing rule has the advantage of administrative convenience; one need produce only a birth certificate to establish a claim to birth citizenship. Under any other rule, individuals would also need to demonstrate the lawful status of a parent at the time of birth, which would often involve intricate legal and documentary inquiries. There would be other difficulties. For example, would children with one citizen parent and one undocumented parent have citizenship at birth? An estimated four million children fit that description as of 2019. For a US immigration bureaucracy that is already taxed by complex immigration rules, additional responsibilities respecting birth citizenship determinations would inevitably lead to administrative error and resource costs.

Limiting birth citizenship to the children of citizens and lawful immigrants creates the possibility of intergenerational caste. If children born to unauthorized immigrants remain for life in the United States, the denial of citizenship creates a mismatch between citizenship allocations and social membership on the ground. This is why the so-called Dreamers have such a powerful claim to citizenship; having entered the United States illegally at an early age, they are as a matter of social fact American in all but name. Denying birth citizenship to the native-born children of unauthorized immigrants would relegate them to a lifetime of legally second-class status. Even if they were extended some form of permanent residence (as Schuck and Smith suggested), they would lack full political equality. (Britain has experienced a similar phenomenon with the so-called Windrush generation, a population of individuals who legally migrated to the United Kingdom from British colonies between 1948 and 1973 but who in many cases lack documentation to establish a claim to citizenship.)

The Supreme Court has never directly ruled that the children of unauthorized immigrants are constitutionally entitled to citizenship at birth, thus leaving the door open to contrary arguments. Perennial efforts to roll back territorial birth citizenship by statute or through a constitutional amendment have gained little traction, failing to pass even initial procedural hurdles at the committee level in Congress.

Candidate Donald Trump deplored birth citizenship as "the biggest magnet for illegal immigration." As president he has since suggested that he could eliminate birth citizenship for the children of unauthorized immigrants by issuing an executive order, without congressional approval. This would circumvent the political impossibility of adopting a constitutional amendment and the political implausibility of passing an applicable statute. The suggestion has provoked strong pushback, including from some conservative writers. Near-absolute territorial birth citizenship is likely to remain US practice into the future.

Does the history of the Fourteenth Amendment support the extension of citizenship to the children of unauthorized immigrants?

The history of the adoption of the Fourteenth Amendment in 1868 is necessarily ambiguous on the question of unauthorized immigrants, insofar as the category did not exist at a time when there were no federal immigration controls—in other words, at a time when there was no such thing as an undocumented immigrant. Some conservatives have argued that as a matter of original intent and consistent with the requirement that citizenship be extended only to those "subject to the jurisdiction" of the United States, the authors of the Fourteenth Amendment would have considered undocumented immigrants beyond the scope of the citizenship clause.

But the historical evidence more likely supports an expansive interpretation. During the floor debates, one legislator inquired of Senator Lyman Trumbull, chairman of the Senate Judiciary Committee and the chief drafter of the amendment, whether the children of Chinese immigrants and "Gypsies" would receive citizenship under the provision. "Undoubtedly," Trumbull replied. Chinese immigrants were barred from naturalization and thus remained subjects of the Chinese emperor, and (as Garrett Epps has shown) the Gypsies were thought to live outside the law in a way resembling today's undocumented immigrants. As highlighted by other colloquies, legislative sponsors of the amendment included the "subject to the jurisdiction thereof" language to carve out the children of foreign diplomats and (far more important) those born into Native American tribes. To the extent the historical record fails to supply a definitive answer, the consistent superseding practice of extending citizenship to all others born on US territory should in any case suffice to overcome any ambiguity in the language and intent of the Fourteenth Amendment in favor of reading it to extend to the children of undocumented immigrants.

Do people born in US territories have citizenship at birth?

Persons born in territories on a path to statehood have always been considered US citizens at birth. Thus, someone born in Arizona before it became a state in 1912 had citizenship at birth. But US territories not on a path to statehood (so-called unincorporated territories) were deemed not to count as the "United States" for purposes of the Fourteenth Amendment. This notion followed the constitutional logic of a series of early twentieth-century decisions known as the *Insular Cases*. Thus, persons born in the Philippines during the period of US sovereign control there did not hold US citizenship. But as for members of Native American tribes, this non-application of the Fourteenth Amendment has been corrected through statutory enactments. Persons born in Puerto Rico, Guam, and the US Virgin Islands have long enjoyed citizenship at birth under these laws.

Even though persons born in US territories have citizenship by statute rather than through the Constitution, as individuals they enjoy all citizenship rights. Persons born in Puerto Rico, for example, can move anywhere in the United States. If resident in one of the fifty states, they are entitled to vote just as are other citizens. As discussed in chapter 3, they may be constitutionally disadvantaged so long as they remain resident in Puerto Rico, but that is also true of any citizen born in one of the fifty states who subsequently relocates to Puerto Rico or another US territory.

American Samoa remains the only US sovereign territory not covered by either the Constitution or a statute for birth citizenship purposes. Persons born in American Samoa carry the anomalous status of "noncitizen national," under which they are entitled to a US passport and international protection but do not enjoy full rights of citizenship. As noncitizen nationals, they are entitled to relocate elsewhere in US territory, but they are denied the vote and are ineligible for some public benefits and public-sector employment. In 2015 a federal appeals court rejected an American Samoan's claim that the Fourteenth Amendment extends to those born in the territory. The refusal to extend citizenship to those born in American Samoa stands as the last surviving example of what was once standard practice among colonial powers.

What are "anchor babies"?

Immigration restrictionists deplore so-called anchor babies as part of their attack on expansive birth citizenship practice in the United States. They argue that noncitizen mothers enter the United States illegally to give birth not simply to secure citizenship for the child, but also to secure legal status for themselves. Because the child has citizenship, the argument runs, the child can then turn around and petition for the legal admission of her parent.

It is true that US citizens can secure the admission of their parents as a general rule. However, under section 201(b) of the Immigration and Nationality Act, a child must turn twenty-one before she can do so. In other words, only twenty-one years after the birth of the citizen child on US territory would a direct advantage accrue to the unauthorized immigrant mother. This statutory timeline largely discredits the "anchor baby" phenomenon as a substantial incentive for unauthorized immigration, notwithstanding the entrenched misconception among restrictionists.

What is "birth tourism"?

Birth tourism describes the phenomenon of pregnant noncitizen women who legally enter the United States intending to give birth for purposes of securing US citizenship for their children. Those who engage in birth tourism are prosperous individuals who can satisfy applicable requirements for tourist visas. An intent to enter the United States to give birth to a child is not by itself a ground for exclusion. Birth tourists tend to be citizens of countries whose passports are less privileged for purposes of international travel, Chinese, Russians, Mexicans, Israelis, and nationals of Middle Eastern countries among them. They often pay significant fees for accommodations and hospital services in the United States. Birth tourism appears to be a growing phenomenon. (It is also on the rise in Canada.) Hospitals have advertised all-inclusive travel packages to noncitizen women for the purpose.

Birth tourism supplies the best argument against the absolute rule of territorial birth citizenship as practiced by the United States. The child who secures citizenship through birth tourism may spend only a couple of weeks in the United States before returning to the mother's country of origin, possibly for life. That child is unlikely to have any social attachment to the United States. The citizenship is procured for purely instrumental purposes, such as securing the ease of international travel that comes with a US passport.

However, the birth tourism phenomenon would by itself hardly justify rolling back territorial birth citizenship. The numbers are still low, almost certainly lower than 100,000 annually. Birth tourism poses few material costs, since those who hold citizenship through birth tourism will typically be nonresident (at least in childhood) and ineligible for public benefits. At worst, holders will avail themselves of the opportunity to relocate to the United States later in life. Since they come from economically well-off families, they are unlikely to implicate the putative costs otherwise associated with immigration. Upending the long-standing practice of territorial birth citizenship would be a disproportionate response to a minor problem.

Birth tourism only works in countries such as the United States and Canada, in which territorial birth is determinative of citizenship. In countries with modified *jus soli* regimes, place of birth by itself will not guarantee citizenship. In the United Kingdom, for example, birth to a noncitizen present on a temporary visa would only result in citizenship if the child thereafter maintained habitual residence until the age of ten. In other countries, the lack of permanent residence status on the mother's part would categorically preclude birth citizenship for the child.

Does a child born abroad get the parent's citizenship?

All countries have some provision for citizenship by descent, so-called *jus sanguinis*. As with many forms of community (religion, for example), national communities are self-replicating through reproduction. In many cases, the children of citizens born outside the country of parental citizenship will have citizenship at birth. The most prevalent form allocates citizenship to children born to parents who were themselves born in the home country and who have maintained their home-country citizenship. A prototypical example is parents who have a baby while temporarily residing outside the home country. Under US law, for example, a child born outside the United States to two citizen parents will have automatic birth citizenship if either parent has resided in the United States at any time prior to the child's birth. If two US citizen parents are working on temporary assignment in, say, Berlin, it makes sense to assume that their child will become part of the American national community.

The rules are more varied and complex when a citizen has a more attenuated connection to the homeland. Historically, it was difficult to maintain homeland citizenship on an intergenerational basis. This was the result of strict rules against dual nationality. To the extent an individual's country of origin prohibited dual citizenship, his or her citizenship by descent would be extinguished upon acquisition of citizenship in another country. For example, European immigrants to the United States in most cases forfeited their home-country nationality for themselves and their descendants when they naturalized in the United States.

As described in chapter 4, many more countries today now accept dual nationality, paving the way for citizenship by descent in a growing number of cases. However, most countries restrict the transmission of citizenship when a family line has been absent from the homeland for more than a generation or two. The bar for citizenship by descent can also be raised when one parent is a citizen and the other a noncitizen. US law requires a continuing territorial connection for citizenship to descend. When two citizens have a child abroad, prior residence of one parent only is required. When a citizen has a child with a noncitizen, the citizen parent must have been physically present in the United States for five years prior to the birth of the child, two of which have to be after the parent reaches age fourteen.

The latter rule has been relaxed from prior requirements. Until 1978, the citizen parent needed ten years of physical presence prior to a child's birth abroad, five of which had to have been after the age of fourteen. (If Barack Obama had been born in Kenya, he would not have had citizenship at birth. His eighteen-year-old citizen mother would not have satisfied the requirement of five years' presence in the United States after the age of fourteen. As with all conspiracy theories, there was a kernel of truth in birtherism—if one could get by the foundational falsehood, that is.) Under the pre-1978 regime, the child born abroad with only one citizen parent also had to satisfy a subsequent requirement of five years' continuous presence herself at some point between the ages of fourteen and twenty-eight. In other words, the child born abroad to only one citizen parent had to return home in order to perfect her citizenship. The US Supreme Court upheld the subsequent presence requirement in its 1971 decision in *Rogers v. Bellei*. Aldo Maria Bellei had acquired citizenship through his Philadelphia-born mother at his birth in 1939 in Italy, thereafter making five short trips to the United States. The Court upheld the cancellation of his citizenship for failure to satisfy the continuous presence requirement.

This presence requirement for the child of the citizen parent was eliminated in 1978, and it is now possible to hold US citizenship from birth to death without ever setting foot in the United States.

Do children born abroad have to "sign up" for citizenship?

Some countries, including the United States, automatically extend citizenship *jus sanguinis* to qualifying individuals. That is, a child born with US citizenship does not have to take any action for purposes of citizenship acquisition. As a result, individuals can discover citizenship they didn't know they had. This can sometimes work to their advantage. Citizenship is an absolute defense to deportation. In many recent cases, individuals with complicated border family histories have been able to establish claims to citizenship in adulthood. (Although the episode involved *jus soli* citizenship, Yaser Hamdi was transferred out of Guantánamo when it was discovered that the alleged Taliban fighter had been born in Louisiana.) US parents who bear a child abroad often secure a Consular Report of Birth Abroad, which serves as prima facie proof of citizenship by descent but is not required for purposes of making a citizenship claim.

Other countries make registration a requirement for *jus sanguinis* citizenship. This orients citizenship to an opt-in model. If parents want to transmit citizenship to a child born abroad (assuming they are otherwise eligible), they must register the child as a citizen with the appropriate diplomatic facility before the child reaches adulthood. Some countries will allow the child herself to make the declaration for some period after becoming an adult if the parents fail to do so. Establishing residence in the home country will in some cases perfect citizenship by descent; that is, if the child born abroad to citizens moves back to the homeland, she will then automatically have citizenship.

What are "accidental Americans"?

Because US citizenship is automatically conferred, whether by territorial birth or parentage, some individuals are deemed US citizens even though they may not have any continuing connection to the United States and may not want the status. For example, a child born to parents who are temporarily present in the United States for work will be extended US citizenship at birth, even if the parents take the child back home in her infancy and she never returns. Similarly, a child born to a US citizen parent abroad may have citizenship at birth even though the parent has permanently resettled and the child is in no way raised as an American. There is no mechanism for rejecting the conferment of citizenship in these cases. Because US citizenship comes with lifelong tax obligations (as described in chapter 3), individuals may have good reason not to want US citizenship. In recent years, some have not discovered they have citizenship until well into adulthood. Under current law, the only way they can shed US citizenship is to go through the ordinary renunciation process, which can be costly and requires payment of back taxes.

When only one parent is a citizen, does it matter whether it is the mother or the father?

Throughout the nineteenth and into the twentieth centuries, under the laws of most countries citizenship descended only through the father. These regimes reflected patriarchal notions of family. They were also aimed at suppressing the incidence of dual nationality; if citizenship were allowed to descend through both mother and father, this argument ran, children would have dual nationality if born to parents of mixed nationality. Under US law, it was not until 1934 that citizenship was deemed to descend through citizen mothers as well as citizen fathers. Sex discrimination in citizenship rules was an early target of international advocacy. In 1933 Western Hemisphere states concluded the Montevideo Convention on the Nationality of Women, which directed ratifying states to end all discrimination on the basis of sex in their nationality practice. Through the middle of the twentieth century many states modified *jus sanguinis* laws to allow citizenship to pass via citizen mothers. Article 9 of the 1979 UN Convention on the Elimination of All Forms of Discrimination Against Women (the Women's Rights Convention) provides that parties "shall grant women equal rights with men with respect to the nationality of their children."

Even though the Women's Rights Convention has been widely ratified (189 countries as of 2018), a number of states attached reservations to their accession with respect to article 9, especially Middle Eastern states; Kuwait, Oman, Saudi Arabia, and Malaysia were among those refusing to modify sex discriminatory *jus sanguinis* regimes. As of 2014, 27 countries continued to maintain provisions preventing mothers from passing citizenship on to their children on the same basis as fathers. The Office of the UN High Commissioner for Refugees has since undertaken a campaign to eliminate this discrimination as part of its efforts to combat statelessness, the risk of which increases when the mother's citizenship does not descend. Since 2003, at least 15 states have conformed *jus sanguinis* laws to sex equality.

When born on an airplane or a ship, what citizenship does one have at birth?

Under article 3 of the 1961 Convention on the Reduction of Statelessness, a person born on an aircraft or ship is considered to be born in the territory of the state whose flag the vessel flies or in which the aircraft is registered, but only if that individual would otherwise be stateless. In other words, a person born on a flag vessel or aircraft may be entitled to that citizenship if entitled to no other citizenship. Otherwise, citizenship will depend on domestic law. Under interpretation of US law, any person born in US airspace is eligible for citizenship on the same basis as a land birth, but birth on a US-registered vessel on the high seas will not qualify. (If birth occurs within US territorial waters, a twelve-mile stretch adjacent to the territorial coasts, one gets US citizenship regardless of what flag the vessel may be flying.) In most cases, the citizenship of a child born aloft or afloat will be determined on a *jus sanguinis* basis, by virtue of the parents' citizenship status.

Do noncitizen children adopted by citizen parents automatically get citizenship?

In the United States, under the Child Citizenship Act of 2000, foreign orphans adopted before the age of sixteen by a US citizen parent automatically receive citizenship upon admission to the United States as a permanent resident. The legislation was adopted in the wake of the deportation of adoptees who had failed to secure naturalization after having engaged in criminal activity long after their admission to the United States. Individuals who had entered the United States in infancy were removed to countries they hardly remembered because their parents had failed to take affirmative steps to secure citizenship for them. Going forward, child adoptees will be immunized from the possibility of deportation through the automatic citizenship grant.

As a mode of citizenship acquisition, automatic citizenship for adoptees is anomalous. It is not classifiable as birth citizenship because it is extended after birth. But because it is automatic, it does not qualify as a form of naturalization. Extending citizenship in these cases seems better to fit the birthright rationale, to the extent that the young adoptee will typically socialize in the United States. (It is an interesting hypothetical to consider whether an adoptee would be eligible to run for president.) Unlike the naturalization applicant, the adoptee will not have any other true country of origin to which he could fairly be repatriated.

How easy is it to demonstrate entitlement to birth citizenship?

In most cases in the developed world, claiming birth citizenship is a relatively straightforward proposition. Entitlement is most easily demonstrated in countries such as the United States and Canada that have absolute rules of *jus soli*. In those countries, production of a valid birth certificate evidencing birth in national territory establishes a claim to citizenship. In developed countries with more restrictive *jus soli* regimes, under which birth citizenship is contingent on the citizenship or immigration status of parents, record-keeping and resident registration practices will usually suffice to establish entitlement to birth citizenship.

In contexts in which documentation is lacking or not accepted as authoritative, birth citizenship claims can be more difficult. Along the southern border of the United States, for example, government authorities have been reluctant to accept certifications of non-hospital midwife deliveries. Entitlement to US citizenship by descent can also be difficult to establish when the duration of physical presence of a parent or grandparent is at issue, in part because the border was once more fluid than it is today.

The problem is much more pervasive in the Global South, where documentation practices have historically been more rudimentary. In the United States, "undocumented" is a euphemism for a person living in the country in violation of immigration laws. In other parts of the world, the description is more literally accurate. There are an estimated forty million unregistered births every year worldwide. Lack of documentation hits indigenous and nomadic peoples particularly hard. The Roma in Europe, for example, often struggle to secure citizenship in the absence of birth registration. In less developed countries, the problem often implicates a lack of state capacity. Hill tribes in Thailand live in villages that may not even be known to state authorities. Members of these tribes may find themselves denied state benefits later in life because they are unable to demonstrate citizenship.

2

NATURALIZATION

Why do countries grant anyone citizenship after birth?

Naturalization implicates the allocation of citizenship after birth. In the conventional template of the modern period, a national of one country who thereafter permanently resettles in another country is able to naturalize in the adopted country. In this migration-centered narrative, naturalization is alternatively considered a reflection of integration into the polity or a tool for perfecting it. In other words, in one perspective naturalization comes after an individual has demonstrated integration, while in another, it facilitates the realization of that end. In either case, it has been in the interest of states to formalize full membership and the rights and responsibilities that have historically been attached to citizenship.

Naturalization remains tied to immigration in most cases, though other aspects of the institution have eroded. It once represented a transfer of loyalty from one sovereign to another. Today, with rising acceptance of dual citizenship, naturalization is much more likely to involve an additional citizenship than a replacement one. More individuals are motivated by the benefits that come with citizenship (especially entry and travel rights), balanced against declining and often nonexistent obligations. States still often have an interest in naturalization not just to recognize membership, but also as a way

Citizenship. Peter J. Spiro, Oxford University Press (2020). © Oxford University Press.
10.1093/actrade/9780190917302.001.0001

to cement ties with useful constituencies. Because naturalization is "achieved" in a different sense than birth citizenship, it opens a window into the meaning of citizenship itself in both contemporary and historical contexts.

What is the history of naturalization?

Ancient Rome extended citizenship on both an individual and a group basis, using it as a key tool in co-opting elites and whole communities as part of imperial expansion. The grant of citizenship in the ancient world did not implicate migration and resettlement or transfer of loyalty from one sovereign to another, but rather conferred status and privilege within a stratified imperial society.

Naturalization in the modern sense was a product of sixteenth-century Britain. As the common law came to allocate nationality on the basis of birthplace, the question emerged of whether those who moved across borders (few as they may have been) were stuck with the significant disabilities of alienage, including limited rights respecting property. On one track, a practice evolved to give the sovereign the power to issue "letters patent of denizenship," under which he could extend to aliens some of the same rights enjoyed by subjects. This status did not operate retroactively and was provisional—it could be revoked as easily as it was granted—and it did not relieve its beneficiaries of some burdens shouldered by aliens, including special taxes.

On another track, Parliament established its authority to naturalize aliens. In an era in which the doctrine of "perpetual allegiance" (described in chapter 4) purported to bind subject and sovereign from birth until death, naturalization involved some metaphysical lifting. As the theory would have it, naturalization was a kind of rebirth; as one English jurist put it, naturalization "hath the like effect that a man's birth hath." The very word "naturalization" (which the modern ear has detached from its linguistic roots) implies as much, as if as a result of the legislative act the individual was somehow made natural, having theretofore been something else.

Naturalization was relatively rare until the eighteenth century. In the United Kingdom it could only be accomplished through legislation particular to the individual, a so-called private bill, involving significant expense and parliamentary investigation of individual merit. It was only in 1709 that a general naturalization process was adopted by Parliament. The law was repealed only three years later in the face of large-scale (for that time) immigration from the conflict-ridden German Palatinate. It was not until 1844 that the United Kingdom again adopted a general naturalization measure. In 1740 the Crown did enable non-British immigrants to the American colonies to naturalize after seven years' residence there, obviating the prior need to secure subject status on British soil. Between 1740 and 1772 almost seven thousand individuals naturalized as British subjects while resident in the colonies.

Have racial and religious criteria been applied to naturalization eligibility?

The United States has a long, disgraceful history of racial qualifications for naturalization extending well into the modern era. The first naturalization law, enacted in 1790, provided for the eligibility of "free whites" only. In the wake of the Civil War and the adoption of the Fourteenth Amendment in 1868, which provided for territorial birthright citizenship, eligibility was extended to "persons of African descent" through the Naturalization Act of 1870. Asians, however, were barred from naturalizing. The 1882 Chinese Exclusion Act expressly barred the "admission" of Chinese to citizenship.

The question of whether individuals of other ethnicities qualified for naturalization gave rise to an unseemly jurisprudence in American courts of the early twentieth century. In its 1922 decision in *Ozawa v. United States*, the Supreme Court rejected the eligibility of Japanese immigrants for naturalization, notwithstanding the "culture and enlighten-ment of the Japanese people." The following year, in *United States v. Thind*, the Court found "a high caste Hindu of full Indian blood" to also be barred even though he was plausibly categorized as "Aryan" by the ethnological categorizations of the day. Both decisions equated "white" persons with those classified as Caucasian as "popularly understood." "It is very far from our thought," the *Thind* Court disingenuously observed, "to suggest the slightest question of racial superi-ority or inferiority," asserting that the Congress was merely recognizing "racial difference" and rejecting "the thought of assimilation." Lower courts subsequently found ineligible individuals from Afghanistan and Arabia, as well as those of mixed Asian and "white" heritage. Immigrants of Hispanic descent generally qualified as "white" and were thus able to naturalize.

The bar on Chinese naturalization was lifted with the repeal of the Chinese Exclusion laws in 1943, driven by the politics of a wartime alliance between the United States and China. Only with the McCarran-Walter Act of 1952 were all racial criteria removed; this act repealed the final bar to persons of Japanese descent. A 1965 immigration statute provided that "[t]he right of a person to become a naturalized citizen of the United States shall not be denied or abridged because of race or sex," a measure that remains on the books today.

Other countries have also imposed racial and ethnic criteria on naturalization, either explicitly or in practice. The *jus san-guinis* regimes that once typified continental European nation-ality regimes effectively excluded most immigrants not sharing the country's dominant ethnicity, though this was leavened by colonial connections through which nonwhites could at times secure citizenship. Naturalization in Liberia and Sierra Leone continues to be restricted to those of "Negro" descent only.

Religious criteria have also been applied to naturaliza-tion eligibility. From 1610 until 1806, UK law required that a would-be subject "receive the sacrament of the Lord's Supper" within one month of naturalization, effectively excluding Catholics and Jews from British nationality. Since 1982 Kuwait has limited naturalization to Muslims. As described later in this chapter, Israeli nationality law privileges Jews who settle in the country.

Do all countries require legal residency as a condition of naturalization?

Exceptional cases aside, almost all countries require some period of residency before an immigrant is eligible to apply for naturalization. (The rule is different for those who naturalize on the basis of ancestry.) Typically, the only residency that counts is that as a permanent resident, that is, after admission as an immigrant. In the United States, for example, a green card is a predicate to citizenship in most cases; one can't skip from a temporary immigration status (for instance, for study or on business) directly to citizenship.

This is all the more true for unauthorized immigrants. Except in very limited circumstances, individuals who are present in a country in violation of immigration laws are ineligible to naturalize. There is a common misunderstanding in the United States at least that unauthorized immigrants can simply sign up for citizenship. It is their failure to do so (often described as laziness) that thereafter makes them subject to deportation. But this is false in the overwhelming majority of cases. Naturalization is predicated on legal permanent residence, which in turn is subject to various threshold qualifications relating to family ties, professional skills, refugee status, or other criteria. Those lacking qualifying characteristics—most of the population desiring to migrate—are ineligible for permanent residence and in turn for citizenship.

Why is a period of residency usually required for naturalization?

The residency period for naturalization is largely subject to the state's discretion. Most states have adopted default residency requirements within a five- to ten-year range. In the United States the default period is five years. Some human rights organizations peg the maximum justifiable period of residency at ten years, as does the 1997 European Convention on Nationality. Nonetheless, some states persist in requiring longer residency periods. India requires twelve years' residence; Eritrea, fifteen years; Qatar, twenty-five years; and the Central African Republic, the outlier, thirty-five years.

Residency is justified on two theories. First is a social control rationale and the notion that a probationary period should be imposed on would-be members. Once an individual acquires citizenship, assuming that naturalization was not acquired on a fraudulent basis, she is absolutely immune from deportation. The residency period without citizenship allows the existing community to revoke the grant of admission if the would-be citizen turns out not to merit permanent membership. In theory this could involve a full vetting of the individual's character for worthiness. In practice, it translates into a window during which an individual can be taken off the citizenship track and physically removed from the country because of post-entry criminal activity.

The social control rationale is coupled with an integration rationale, on the theory that some period of residency is necessary for an individual to integrate sufficiently to become a full, permanent member of the political community. Individuals need to spend time rubbing shoulders—almost literally—with their would-be compatriots before exercising rights of political participation. During the residency period, the theory holds, individuals will absorb the sociopolitical understandings of a national community. This reflects a conception of naturalization under which the acquisition of citizenship reflects rather than facilitates social membership. Once an immigrant has satisfied the requisite residency period, she will be a member of the community as a matter of social fact. The grant of citizenship, backstopped by language and civics-related requirements, will validate what has already happened on the ground.

Do some naturalization applicants get preferential treatment?

States often extend preferences and/or exemptions to certain groups with respect to naturalization requirements. For example, some individuals are subject to reduced residency requirements. Many countries reduce the residency threshold for the immigrant spouses of existing citizens. In the United States the usual five-year period is reduced to three if an applicant lives with a citizen spouse. In Malaysia, to cite another example, only two years' residency is required for spouses, as opposed to the usual eleven. The reduction can be justified insofar as proximity to an existing citizen will accelerate integration of the prospective naturalization applicant. It's a kind of pillow-talk fast track. In some countries, for example France and the Netherlands, cohabiting with a citizen-spouse counts even if it is outside the country; in other words, it substitutes for rather than merely reduces the residency requirement.

Most Latin American states, along with Spain, reduce the applicable residency requirements for their citizens on a reciprocal basis. Immigrants who are citizens of Latin America need reside in Spain for only two years, compared to the usual ten for others. In theory, this reflects the historical affinities between and among Spain and its former colonial possessions. Immigrants from a Hispanic culture will require a lesser period of shoulder-rubbing with existing citizens on the way to social integration. But the practice results in a serious disadvantage for non-Hispanic immigrants. In Spain, many immigrants from North Africa are subject to the higher barrier. The differential may seem benign—an expression of national identity—but the result is discriminatory in ways that correlate to race.

For many years Germany's naturalization regime included a special provision for the so-called *Aussiedler*, ethnic Germans (those who "belong to the German people") who had settled in Eastern Europe and Central Asia as far back as the sixteenth century. To qualify for the status, immigrants were only required to demonstrate German ethnicity; there were no additional requirements relating to language or cultural knowledge. Many *Aussiedler* had no German identity beyond their surnames. During the Cold War, *Aussiedler* were limited by East Bloc exit restrictions, but with the fall of the Iron Curtain a trickle became a wave. More than 4.5 million immigrants availed themselves of automatic citizenship upon relocation to Germany. The program became controversial because it extended citizenship to individuals with no real ties to Germany at the same time that long-term Turkish and other immigrants resident in Germany were blocked from naturalization. In 1993 the *Aussiedler* preference was eliminated; those born before 1993 were grandfathered in, while other individuals from Eastern European states were required to demonstrate that their German ethnicity had resulted in persecution.

What is Israel's Law of Return?

Under Israel's Law of Return, adopted in 1950 soon after the country secured independence, any Jew who has expressed a desire to settle in Israel is entitled to settlement. Jews who acquire citizenship under the law are not considered immigrants but rather repatriates (hence the law's title). The law is considered constitutive of the Israeli state. It was adopted by acclamation as implementing the concept of Aliyah, which means "ascent" in Hebrew.

The Law of Return has been contested on the question of who qualifies as Jewish for purposes of eligibility. In 1970 the law was amended to provide that "for the purposes of this Law, 'Jew' means a person who was born of a Jewish mother or has become converted to Judaism and who is not a member of another religion," thus conforming the nationality regime to the religion's matrilineal orientation. Because the law defines eligibility on the basis of descent, however, it is possible for individuals to avail themselves of Israeli nationality even if they do not practice Judaism. An estimated 400,000 non-observant Jewish immigrants entered Israel after 1989 from the former Soviet Union on the basis of ancestral, not religious, qualifications.

Obviously the Law of Return privileges people on the basis of religion. Defenders highlight Israel's identity as the Jewish state. Detractors frame the regime as discriminatory against others. Non-Jews who immigrate to Israel are required to satisfy ordinary naturalization requirements, including capacity in the Hebrew language. (Those born in Israel to at least one Israeli citizen receive Israeli citizenship at birth, regardless of religious ancestry. Approximately 20 percent of Israeli citizens are of Arab ethnicity.) The differential faced by some non-Jews has grown starker since 2002, when, in the wake of the second Intifada, Palestinians were made ineligible to naturalize even if they married Israeli citizens. The Law of Return has been denounced by some international human rights agencies as discriminatory.

What is the so-called citizenship test for US naturalization?

Name one branch of government. In what month do we vote for president? How many justices are on the Supreme Court? Who did the United States fight in World War II? What did Martin Luther King Jr. do? Name your representative in Congress. What stops one branch of government from becoming too powerful? What ocean is on the East Coast of the United States? These are among the hundred questions from which ten are drawn for each US naturalization applicant. Answering six of the ten correctly satisfies the so-called civics requirement.

Under US law, naturalization applicants are required to "demonstrate a knowledge and understanding of the fundamentals of the history, and of the principles and form of government, of the United States." Congress adopted the civics requirement in 1950, before which judges would sometimes quiz applicants on their knowledge of constitutional principles on the way to administering the naturalization oath.

In theory, a naturalization test could measure social integration and fitness to participate responsibly in the political system. It might also represent a sort of rite of passage, as part of which naturalizing citizens can feel a sense of accomplishment in successfully pursuing naturalization. But the current US test is mostly an exercise in rote memorization. One can satisfy the requirement without having any real understanding of US history or government. The elementary geography aside, the official study guide supplies short answers to the more conceptual questions. ("Checks and balances" is the right answer to the question about what stops one branch of government from becoming too powerful.) Observers have lamented the execution of the civics requirement for decades, and during the 1990s and early 2000s the immigration agency convened expert groups to consider an overhaul of the test. In the end, the revised version issued in 2006 fiddled around the edges, retaining the sample question/short answer format. Some questions were changed, but not in any meaningful way. A question about Patrick Henry was dropped; one about Benjamin Franklin was added.

Only those with developmental disabilities or mental impairments are exempted from the civics requirement. It is a deterrent for some would-be applicants. Although the questions seem simple, especially since they are available in advance, for immigrants of limited education taking any sort of test can be intimidating. A persistent rumor that failure will result in deportation doesn't help. Applicants over age sixty-five who have resided in the United States for at least twenty years are tested on a subset of the one hundred sample questions, pursuant to the statute's command that they be given "special consideration." Those who are exempted from the language requirement can take the test in their native tongue.

Do other countries have citizenship tests?

Other countries place emphasis on the everyday elements of social membership in their naturalization exams. Those naturalizing in the United Kingdom must pass the "Life in the UK" test, pursuant to a 2005 statute requiring applicants to show "sufficient knowledge of life in the United Kingdom." As on the US test, many of the questions (applicants must answer eighteen of twenty-four questions correctly) involve history, geography, and political institutions. Some are quite elementary ("What is the capital of the United Kingdom?"); others are intuitive ("There is no place in British society for extremism or intolerance"—true or false?); and others simply have to be learned (the date of the Battle of Bosworth Field or when women were given an equal right to vote). But the UK naturalization process also looks to test the applicant's understanding of social customs and how to get around. There are questions about Valentine's Day, pub opening times, and what people eat on Christmas Day.

Although most questions highlight the white, Anglican, monarchical elements of British society, there are also questions about Ramadan, Hanukkah, and the Sikh festival Vaisakhi. Applicants are tested on how to look for work, paying taxes, and the national insurance system. (The first version of the test was criticized for including contested material on "everyday needs," including the appropriate response to spilling beer on someone in a pub.) Unlike the US test, material on which the questions are based is available beforehand, but not the questions themselves. The pass rate for the UK test is low— around a third of test-takers fail—but naturalization applicants can repeat the test as many times as it takes to pass (though they have to pay £50 for each try).

Germany once dispatched naturalization "inspectors" to applicants' homes to see if they were fully assimilated as Germans. The joke was (perhaps only half in jest) that one had to have Schiller on the bookcase to satisfy the acculturation requirement, and indeed discretionary naturalization was not commonly granted. Today, Germany administers a test similar to those of other countries. As in the British approach, applicants for German naturalization need to show adequate knowledge of the German way of life. Dutch "integration requirements" specify language capacity and knowledge of Dutch society, including cultural mores. (Those seeking permanent residence in the Netherlands, not just naturalization applicants, must now also pass the test.) Those holding certain diplomas or certificates (not all of them academic) may be exempted. The pass rate for the Dutch integration exam is around 75 percent. In Germany, it is over 90 percent. Other European countries can be tougher. The fail rate in Denmark as of 2016 was around 70 percent, with questions such as "Which Danish restaurant gained its third Michelin star in February 2016?" appearing on the test.

Some countries supplement the test with a requirement that naturalization applicants enroll in integration courses. In Europe these courses are substantial, with instruction ranging from four hundred to nine hundred hours. These courses are devoted mostly to preparing prospective applicants for the language sufficiency requirements that are coupled with the civics test. In some countries, successful completion of an integration test satisfies the civics requirements.

Are naturalization exams justifiable?

Naturalization tests can be justified as a way to both assess and facilitate social membership. Each country has its distinctive characteristics, its citizenry understanding a distinctive data set. New citizens, the argument runs, need to share that knowledge as a condition to full, permanent membership. To the extent the tests focus on a country's governmental processes, moreover, they can also measure whether an immigrant is equipped to exercise responsible political participation.

But testing requirements are in tension with liberal values. Those who can't pass the test are denied equality and political rights in the country in which they may have lived for some number of years. This is akin to the pre–civil rights era practice in the United States of administering literacy tests at polling places as a way to exclude African Americans from the franchise. Nor does the premise of a common data set shared by the existing citizenry map onto reality. Many studies in the United States have shown that native-born Americans—even highly educated ones—would fail the US citizenship test. (Some US states have sought to fix this by making successful completion of the naturalization test a requirement for high school graduation, but the knowledge gained would be only as good as the memorization required.) To the extent citizens share common knowledge, moreover, it is more likely to be global than national. In other words, national understandings, customs, and even politics are no longer distinctive. This will make sustained imposition of the citizenship test challenging in most countries and more difficult over time.

Is naturalization contingent on language facility?

Most countries require some level of proficiency in a dominant or official language as a predicate to naturalization. In the United States there was no language qualification for naturalization before the early twentieth century. A 1905 commission that President Theodore Roosevelt charged with proposing reforms to the naturalization process found it "incontrovertible that no man is a desirable citizen of the United States who does not know the English language." Congress adopted legislation the following year denying naturalization to those "who cannot speak the English language." In 1952 the requirement was modified to require an "understanding" of

English, defined as including "an ability to read, write, and speak words in ordinary usage in the English language." This remains a part of the nationality law today.

Language facility is folded into the civics test, which is administered in English and for which the naturalization examiner will require the applicant to read some questions out loud and answer some questions in writing. The statute exempts older long-term residents from the language requirement (those over age fifty who have been resident for at least twenty years and those over age fifty-five who have been resident at least fifteen years). These applicants still have to pass the civics test administered in their native language. As with the civics requirements, those with mental or developmental disabilities are exempted from the language requirement.

The US approach requires only rudimentary language skills. Other countries require a higher level of language facility. In 2013 the United Kingdom raised its language requirement to English B1, which is described as "the ability to express oneself in a limited way in familiar situations and to deal in a general way with nonroutine information." For example, applicants must be able to "describe experiences and events, dreams, hopes and ambitions and briefly give reasons and explanations for opinions and plans." Although Germany no longer requires fluency, applicants must be "able to cope in German with daily life in Germany, including dealing with the authorities."

Language requirements are subject to the same sort of critique as civics tests. In the United States the language requirement seems particularly problematic, since there is no official national language, and in many areas of the country one can be a fully functioning member of the community without having English-language facility (Spanish being the obvious alternative). Knowledge of English may once have been necessary for full political participation. Today, prospective voters can fully inform themselves through non-English-language media—a kind of back-to-the-future of immigrant-rich nineteenth-century America. New citizens don't even need English to execute the franchise. Under the Voting Rights Act, ballots must be printed in any language used by 5 percent of the voting age population in any electoral jurisdiction.

The argument for the language requirement may be stronger in countries with linguistically homogenous traditions. Even in the United States, where English is the dominant language, would-be citizens are more likely to be fully integrated members of society. But those applicants who are unable to satisfy language requirements will be deprived of those rights that distinctively attach to citizenship, including full political equality. On that measure, language tests may trammel liberal values.

Do would-be citizens have to show they are good people?

In the United States, naturalization applicants have since the first naturalization law in 1790 been required to demonstrate "good moral character" during the requisite residency period. At one time the condition was interpreted as barring naturalization for any violation of law, even if the violation was not prosecuted. In the early twentieth century there were cases in which judges denied naturalization for a single act of adultery, possession of intoxicating liquor (during Prohibition), failure to support a child born out of wedlock, and even traffic violations. Judges had discretion to apply the character requirement as they saw fit, often in combination with the parallel requirement (also included in the first naturalization law and since) that applicants demonstrate "attachment to the principles of the Constitution."

Good moral character was later defined in 1952 legislation to exclude individuals convicted of "crimes of moral turpitude" and offenses connected to controlled substances, as well as so-called aggravated felonies. These are mostly moot for naturalization purposes because they will also result in deportation (in other words, the individual won't be allowed to stay in the country, much less acquire citizenship). The character requirement is now mostly interpreted to allow naturalization in the absence of criminality—that is, as long as the applicant has not been convicted of criminal offenses. The statutory definition does, however, continue to include some morals-related exclusions. Until 1981 a finding of good moral character was precluded for any applicant who had committed adultery during the requisite residency period. Even today, one whose "income is principally derived from illegal gambling activities" is barred from naturalization, even without a conviction. In 2017 a federal appeals court upheld the denial of naturalization for an applicant who was conceded to be "a habitual drunkard." This remains a statutory preclusion to a showing of good character.

Most other countries also require good character and/or preclude naturalization on the basis of criminal history. In Angola applicants cannot have been convicted of a crime punishable by more than three years in prison. Sweden requires that applicants have led and can be expected to lead a "respectable life." Saudi Arabia bars naturalization of applicants who are "crazy or insane," per the law's official translation. In recent years some countries have adopted requirements related to financial self-sufficiency. In Denmark, for instance, individuals must demonstrate that they have been self-supporting for four and a half out of the five years preceding the citizenship application.

Finally, naturalization isn't free. In most countries applicants must pay a fee, in some cases a steep one. In the United States applicants must pay $725, with no discount for dependents. For a family of four, the cost runs to almost $3,000, a significant burden for an average middle-class immigrant family. The cost has more than doubled over the past decade. Waivers are available in cases of financial need, but waiver requests involve an additional level of bureaucracy and delay. The ordinary fee for naturalization in the United Kingdom is more than £1,300, with a small discount for those under age eighteen. These fee levels are at the higher end; in Belgium, France, Germany, and other countries, the cost is less than $100 per applicant. In the United States and United Kingdom, high fees are justified as covering administrative costs. But the high cost may scare some eligible applicants away. Some immigrants aren't securing citizenship and the rights that come with it simply because it costs too much.

What is the citizenship oath?

Some countries require the taking of an oath as a requirement for naturalization. The United States, for example, requires applicants to declare

> that I absolutely and entirely renounce and abjure all allegiance and fidelity to any foreign prince, potentate, state, or sovereignty, of whom or which I have heretofore been a subject or citizen; that I will support and defend the Constitution and laws of the United States of America against all enemies, foreign and domestic; that I will bear true faith and allegiance to the same; that I will bear arms on behalf of the United States when required by the law [or] that I will perform noncombatant service in the Armed Forces of the United States when required by the law.

The oath is largely unchanged since 1795, which explains the archaic phrasing. It was long mandatory in all cases. In 2000, in response to cases in which permanent residents suffering from dementia were blocked from naturalizing (and thus ineligible for certain public benefits) because they could not understand the nature of the oath they were taking, a waiver from the requirement was made possible where an otherwise eligible individual suffers from a developmental disability or mental impairment.

The oath is administered at the end of the naturalization process. In the public perception, these ceremonies are presided over by federal judges and other dignitaries eloquently declaiming the value of citizenship. The media give play to elaborate ceremonies staged every July 4th. But most new US citizens are sworn in by low-level bureaucrats in government offices, followed by a video message from the president (in 2019, from one who is famously immigrant unfriendly). The dignity of these ceremonies is only one step above getting a driver's license.

Other countries have adopted updated, more modern citizenship oaths. Naturalizing Australians, for example, "pledge" their "loyalty to Australia and its people, whose democratic beliefs I share, whose rights and liberties I respect, and whose laws I will uphold and obey," and nothing further. In Germany, naturalizing citizens are required to declare that they will respect the country's laws. Oaths were historically important in Western Hemisphere states, reflecting their immigrant origins and the perceived need, in the nineteenth century at least, to solemnize the transfer of allegiance from one country to another. As US attorney general Jeremiah Black observed in 1859, if the oath of renunciation "did not work a dissolution of every political tie which bound him to his native country, then our naturalization laws are a bitter mockery and the oath we administer to foreigners is a delusion and a snare." Most naturalization oaths focus on loyalty to country and an undertaking to observe the laws of the state. In an effort to revive the meaning of citizenship, the United Kingdom undertook naturalization ceremonies for the first time in 2004.

Citizenship oaths do not present a particularly significant barrier to naturalization. But some would-be US citizens are deterred by the oath's renunciation requirement, even though termination of prior nationality has never been enforced, attorney general Black's position notwithstanding. The Australian oath once required applicants to swear allegiance to Elizabeth II as queen of Australia (as continues to be true of the Canadian oath and those of most other Commonwealth countries). When that element was removed in 1994, there was a spike in naturalization applications, apparently explained by a number of Irish immigrants who, though otherwise eligible, refused to make the symbolic bow to the British monarch. An Irish immigrant to Canada recently launched an unsuccessful legal challenge to that country's continued requirement that new citizens swear allegiance to the queen.

If unauthorized immigrants are legalized in the United States, should they get a "path to citizenship"?

For the past decade, intense immigration reform debates in the United States have centered on the status of a large, long-standing population of unauthorized immigrants, estimated at eleven to thirteen million individuals. At stake is whether the immigration status of this population, or some subset thereof, should be regularized to make their presence in the United States legal. A touchstone of these debates is whether this legalization should include a "path to citizenship." The discourse assumes that unauthorized immigrants whose presence is regularized should be eligible to secure citizenship and full equality in the polity.

Recent proposals would add more hurdles, so that beneficiaries would not immediately be eligible for permanent resident status and an ordinary track to naturalization (five years in most cases). A 2013 compromise proposal by the so-called Gang of Eight (senators from both parties who attempted to break a legislative logjam on comprehensive immigration reform) would have extended a probationary legal status to unauthorized immigrants. Permanent residency would have been available to these beneficiaries only after they had paid back taxes, demonstrated a work history in the United States, and learned English and civics. The proposal thus took some naturalization requirements and made them a hurdle to permanent residency. The last major regularization of unauthorized immigrants was the Immigration Reform and Control Act of 1986. It supplied a limited precedent, to the extent that it required applicants for permanent residency to show that they were "pursuing a course of study to achieve" the English and civics requirements. The most recent cycle of debate would harden those requirements.

Some have suggested that legalization should preclude the possibility of naturalization, in other words, that beneficiaries should not be afforded any path to citizenship. This points to the possibility of a "permanent noncitizen resident" category consisting of those unauthorized immigrants whose status is regularized. The concept enjoys some support in polls, including among putative beneficiaries. This is not surprising. Unauthorized immigrants care most about their insecure status with respect to work and presence. But permanent noncitizenship status would challenge American political culture to the extent that it would provide for permanent second-class status. It is unlikely to be a component of immigration reform. It is nonetheless possible that the path to citizenship could be a very long one.

The concept of permanent noncitizen status is less alien in some other states. In Latvia, ethnic Russians resident in the territory at the time of the breakup of the Soviet Union unable to qualify for citizenship under ordinary naturalization requirements were extended a noncitizen resident status (including a passport as such). In countries with formerly onerous naturalization requirements such as Germany, immigrants often had no opportunity as a practical matter to acquire citizenship. At the same time they were typically eligible for all social benefits; they were denied political rights only.

Can one buy citizenship?

An increasing number of countries have put citizenship up for sale. Countries allowing naturalization via investment and/or direct monetary contribution include a number of Caribbean states, Cyprus, and Malta. Real estate is a common qualifying investment. Prices vary. One can buy citizenship in Dominica for under $100,000. In St. Kitts and Nevis, prospective citizens can choose between a non-refundable donation of $150,000 to its sustainable growth fund or property investment of at least $200,000. The European programs are more expensive. In Malta, applicants must make a contribution of €650,000 to a national development fund, invest at least €350,000 in property, and purchase 150,000 euros' worth of government bonds.

The investment/sale route to citizenship has triggered some controversy. Forerunners in the 1980s, including in Belize and a number of Pacific Island states, were plagued by corruption. Some programs were exploited by nefarious types looking to evade law enforcement or skip out on tax bills. Other countries saw little return on the proceeds. Tonga lost more than $20 million it had sold in passports at $20,000 each when it was scammed by an American money manager. The manager held the official position of court jester to the island nation's king.

These issues have largely been addressed in the current generation of investor citizenship programs. The programs have been outsourced and professionalized. A Swiss-based firm, Henley & Partners, has helped several countries, including St. Kitts and Malta, establish their programs. Brokers have helped countries market their programs to wealth advisers, accountants, and others who service a growing global population of high-net-worth individuals; they also help to screen prospective applicants for criminal activity and other disqualifying conditions. It's a kind of franchise system around which an industry has emerged. These professionals have a vested interest in keeping the investor citizenship programs "clean."

Demand for investor citizenship is growing among wealthy individuals from countries that do not enjoy high levels of visa-free travel to developed countries. Russian, Chinese, and Middle Eastern multimillionaires still need a visa to travel to the European Union. With a passport from Malta, they enjoy the right not only to travel freely within the EU and the United States but also to settle in any EU member state. Buyers rarely secure investor citizenship to reside in the state issuing the passport; those purchasing Maltese citizenship, for example, don't mean to live there. Even a St. Kitts passport comes with visa-free travel to the EU, secured through efforts undertaken not so much by St. Kittian diplomats as by self-interested representatives of the broker companies.

The programs remain controversial even as they are being routinized. The EU's European Commission vigorously objected to Malta's initial proposal, under which citizenship would have been granted upon approval of the application. Although it was able to secure from Malta a one-year nominal residency requirement (which can be established with gym club memberships and the like; actual presence is not required), in the end the commission lacked the authority to veto the program under EU law.

Theorists have also been agitated by the programs insofar as they challenge traditional conceptions that equate citizenship with social membership. As Ayelet Shachar argues, investor citizenship "may cause irreparable harm to the vision of citizenship as grounded in long-term relations of trust and shared responsibility and may prefigure the conflation of the political and ethical with the economic and calculative." This "red-carpet citizenship," she argues, undermines the "basic egalitarian and participatory thrust of political membership as we currently know it."

No doubt investor citizenship raises valid equality concerns, as more fully explored in chapter 6. But there is no international legal impediment to the sale of citizenship. For smaller states such as Malta, investor citizenship significantly bolsters annual government revenue, and the incentives to sustain the program are thus significant. Although there may be price competition as more states enter the market, investor citizenship is probably here to stay.

This is not to say that it will be accepted in all iterations. In one particularly controversial case, the United Arab Emirates purchased citizenship in bulk from the Comoros Islands to be distributed to the UAE's stateless Bidoon population, a community of tens of thousands born and habitually resident in the UAE. The transaction involved shady middlemen and suitcases full of cash exchanged for suitcases full of blank passports. From the UAE's perspective, the availability of Comoros citizenship answered human rights objections to the Bidoons' stateless status. Many Bidoons have accepted the offered passports to facilitate international travel even though they have no connection to the Comoros, a cash-strapped, non-destination island group in the Indian Ocean. Even when Bidoons accept citizenship, they are apparently not entitled to travel to the Comoros. It's not clear that this maneuver will stick. The United States, for one, refuses to accept the validity of passports issued to the Bidoons, and human rights groups have condemned the move.

Many more states offer permanent residence status to investing immigrants. Under the so-called EB-5 program, for example, individuals can secure US green cards in return for investments as low as $500,000. The United Kingdom, Portugal, and Greece also offer such programs. (Canada scaled back its investor residence program in 2014, as few subscribers established roots in the country.) These "golden visas" have been controversial for many of the same reasons that apply to investor citizenship programs. Although they do not directly lead to naturalization, in some cases they reduce naturalization requirements. For example, while immigrant investors to Portugal are subject to the standard six-year residency requirement for naturalization, they need to be physically present in Portugal only seven days during each of those years. Bulgaria shortens its usual ten-year residency requirement to two years for some golden visa holders. Bulgarian citizenship may not sound like much, but with Bulgarian citizenship comes all the travel and settlement rights of citizenship in the EU.

Do states sometimes extend citizenship to individuals with special talents?

A number of states allow fast-track naturalization for immigrants who have benefited or are expected to benefit the state in some extraordinary way. For example, immigrants are eligible for citizenship in the Czech Republic if their naturalization would result in great benefit to the country in the fields of science, education, culture, or sports. Other states where naturalization is available to talented individuals (usually with a waiver of residency, language, and other standard naturalization requirements) include Canada, Brazil, the Netherlands, Italy, Indonesia, Morocco, and Madagascar. The United States and United Kingdom are among those states lacking such special naturalization provisions. (Both countries do have special visa categories for immigrants of exceptional ability, who then have to comply with ordinary requirements for naturalization.)

Although such provisions are often restricted to those with exceptional talent, in some countries any special benefit rendered to the state enables the grant of citizenship. Twenty-two-year-old Mamoudou Gassama, an unauthorized immigrant from Mali, was extended French citizenship in 2018 after heroically scaling a building to save a boy who was dangling from a fourth-floor balcony. Another Malian was granted citizenship after hiding several shoppers from an attacker in a Jewish supermarket in Paris in 2015.

Among the talented, sports figures are the most prominent beneficiaries. For the Olympics and other major international sporting competitions, athletes are required to have the nationality of the states for which they compete. To the extent countries are looking to recruit foreign talent for their teams, citizenship is a necessary part of the package. Special public service naturalization provisions allow states to include foreigners on team rosters without the wait times imposed on other applicants for naturalization.

Vladimir Putin has exercised his authority to extend Russian citizenship to advance the country's competitiveness in sports. Beneficiaries have included US basketball players Becky Hammon and J. R. Holden, both of whom were issued Russian passports so they could compete with the Russian team at the 2008 Olympics. Short-track speed skater Viktor Ahn received special naturalization in time for the 2014 Winter Games in Sochi, before which he switched from the South Korean to the Russian team. None of these athletes was required to live in Russia or learn the Russian language prior to acquiring citizenship, as they would have been if subject to ordinary naturalization rules. Neither Kylie Dickson nor Alaina Kwan, both American-born gymnasts, even visited the former Soviet republic Belarus before being granted citizenship by and competing for that country in the 2016 Rio Games.

Does military service result in citizenship?

Similarly to individuals whose naturalization would specially benefit the state, noncitizens who enlist in the armed services are sometimes afforded a fast track to citizenship. Under US law, noncitizens are eligible to naturalize after a single year of military service, none of which need be in the United States, instead of the usual five-year residency requirement. In designated periods of hostilities, eligibility for naturalization is immediate upon enlistment.

Both world wars, along with the Korean and Vietnam conflicts, qualified as periods of hostilities for naturalization purposes. In a July 2002 executive order, President George W. Bush designated the period beginning with the September 11, 2001 terrorist attacks as triggering the provision. That 2002 order remains in effect. Noncitizens comprise an estimated 3 to

4 percent of enlisted personnel in the US armed forces. Since the 2002 action, the United States has naturalized more than 125,000 members of the military. Almost 10 percent of these naturalizing citizens were sworn in overseas, the only context in which naturalization is authorized outside the territorial United States. Also unique to the US naturalization regime, eligibility is not contingent on permanent residence status, although the naturalization of legal non-immigrants is uncommon, to the extent that permanent residence is almost always a condition of enlistment. (A small pilot program to recruit noncitizens with critical language and other skills—the Military Accessions Vital to the National Interest program, MAVNI—allowed those on student visas and other temporary immigrants to access citizenship directly, but the program has been administratively strangled by the Trump administration.) Under the statute, naturalization can be revoked if an individual is dishonorably discharged before completing five years' duty.

Other countries also eliminate residency requirements for noncitizens serving in the military, though few others establish eligibility immediately upon enlistment. Those who serve in the French Foreign Legion are eligible after three years' service, in place of the ordinary five years' residence. In Canada, enlistees are eligible after two years rather than the usual five.

Beginning in 1990, US law has provided for posthumous awards of citizenship to noncitizens killed as a result of military service. Fifty-nine individuals who died while on active duty have been granted posthumous citizenship. While this is only symbolic for the dead service member, durational residency requirements are waived for surviving spouses and children who wish to naturalize.

Can countries naturalize whomever they want?

As a general matter, states have full discretion to grant citizenship to whomever they wish on whatever basis. They are under no obligation to impose any of the typical requirements for naturalization. Even though most states require residency as a condition for naturalization, they don't have to. This discretion enables investor and Olympic citizenship, as discussed previously.

However, naturalization can only occur on a volition basis, that is, only with an individual's consent. One has to apply for naturalization; it can't be imposed. To take one hypothetical, Canada couldn't enact a naturalization measure deeming all residents of Detroit to be Canadian citizens. As a blue-ribbon Harvard-based commission observed in 1929, "the general principle that no state is free to acquire the allegiance of natural persons without their consent is believed to be generally recognized." It continued: "If State A should attempt . . . to naturalize persons who have never had any connection with State A, who have never been within its territory, who have never acted in its territory, who have no relation whatever to any persons who have been its nationals, and who are nationals of other states, it would seem that State A would clearly have gone beyond the limits set by international law."

The consent principle may seem obvious, but it wasn't always so. During the nineteenth century several Latin American countries attempted to automatically extend nationality on the basis of residence or the ownership of real estate. The measure was aimed at depriving Americans and Europeans doing business in Latin America of the protection of their home governments. The United States and European countries successfully pushed back against these measures, which gave rise to the international norm.

Today, with the exception of extending citizenship to the minor children of naturalization applicants (so-called derivative naturalization), no state imposes naturalization by operation of law. However, there are recent cases implicating the norm in which citizenship has been effectively imposed under duress. The example of the United Arab Emirates buying Comoros citizenship for the otherwise stateless Bidoons is one such case. Some Bidoons have accepted Comoros passports, even though they have no connection to that country, by way of securing a travel document; any passport is better than none. But they can hardly be said to have accepted Comoros nationality of their own accord. More notable is Russia's mass naturalization of residents of the Crimea after it occupied the territory in 2014. Russia adopted a law under which residents of Crimea were made citizens of the Russian Federation unless they opted out. The opt-out period lasted only eighteen days; those looking to reject Russian citizenship faced logistical and bureaucratic obstacles. Moreover, those who opted out are considered foreigners and therefore left at the mercy of an arbitrarily administered system for residency permits. The UN General Assembly, UN High Commissioner for Refugees, and human rights groups have condemned Russia's action as an "automatic naturalization" of Crimeans.

What was the Nottebohm Case?

Even if states are largely unconstrained in extending citizenship as they please, such action doesn't always translate into international effect. The International Court of Justice rejected the capacity of a state to exercise diplomatic protection on behalf of a national with whom it lacked a "social fact of attachment" in its 1955 ruling in the *Nottebohm Case*, easily the most notable ruling from an international tribunal on a nationality-related question.

The case involved Guatemala's detention of Friedrich Nottebohm and the expropriation of his property in 1943. Nottebohm had been born in Germany in 1881 as a German national but had long lived in Guatemala. In 1939 he naturalized in Liechtenstein, even though he had never lived and there and continued his residence in Guatemala. His German nationality was extinguished when he naturalized in another country. Guatemala continued to treat him as a German and expropriated his property as that of an enemy alien after the country entered World War II on the side of the Allies.

The World Court rejected Liechtenstein's attempt to assert a claim against Guatemala on behalf of its national relating to the expropriation of his property, on the grounds that Nottebohm had insufficient ties to Liechtenstein. *Nottebohm* stands for the proposition, some argue, that citizenship must be founded on "genuine links" between the individual and the state. Others interpret the decision narrowly to apply only to claims before international tribunals. By its own terms, the ruling did not challenge Liechtenstein's capacity to naturalize Nottebohm on its own terms for purposes of its own law. In any case, in today's world it is increasingly difficult to pinpoint the meaning of "genuine links" as a meaningful hurdle.

Do all eligible immigrants naturalize?

Not all immigrants acquire citizenship even when they have satisfied the requisite residency period. The explanations for this "denizen" population are contingent on country conditions. Naturalization will always involve affirmative action on an individual's part. That is, the individual has to come forward to apply for the status, even when the requirements are minimal. In some countries, naturalization requirements are arduous. It may not be easy, for example, to learn the language of the country of resettlement at the level required for naturalization. In other cases, it may not seem worth the effort even if the naturalization requirements are not especially onerous. In all cases, naturalization involves some interaction with immigration authorities and the hassles that may involve. Citizenship may not include significant additional rights. As discussed in chapter 4, individuals with citizenship are primarily advantaged with respect to voting rights and absolute insulation from deportation. Those additional rights, however meaningful, may not suffice as incentives to overcome the inertia, expense, and effort involved in naturalization.

Other disincentives may come into play. Some countries of origin terminate citizenship when an individual naturalizes in another state. In those cases, forfeiting birth citizenship becomes a price of naturalization. Even if a person has permanently resettled and retains little practical need for her original citizenship, the sentimental value of original citizenship may remain high—too high to justify what may be the incremental advantages of naturalization.

Even where the loss of original citizenship is not part of the picture—as for citizens of the increasing number of states accepting dual citizenship—some permanent residents do not want to take the symbolic step of acquiring citizenship in the country in which they live but to which they do not feel an emotional attachment. This became evident in the United States during the presidency of George W. Bush and even more so during the Donald Trump years. Europeans living permanently in the United States may be committed to their localities, especially in coastal cities, and intend to live out their days as residents of the United States. But they do not want to take the expressive step of pledging loyalty to a country whose governmental policies they may abhor.

Finally, the state itself plays an important role in facilitating naturalization. While all states impose some barriers in the form of naturalization requirements, they can be more or less facilitative of naturalization for those in a position to qualify. Some states, for example, offer free language and civics classes for prospective naturalization applicants. Sociologist Irene Bloemraad finds that such integration policies explain why Canada has a significantly higher naturalization rate than the United States.

Who administers naturalization?

In most countries, naturalization is administered by national authorities. In some federal states, however, provincial governments or their equivalent have had responsibility for executing naturalization laws. In the United States, immigrants were naturalized mostly by state court judges until 1906. The process was exploited by urban political machines to pad electoral rolls with new voters. Congress responded with legislation giving the federal courts exclusive jurisdiction over naturalization.

In Germany the provincial Länder remain responsible for processing naturalization applications. For a brief period during the 2000s, the Länder were able to require civics tests for naturalization and had the authority to formulate questions. In other words, whether and what kind of naturalization exam applicants had to pass varied by province. That authority was retracted after some Länder adopted questions with a clear anti-Muslim bias in tests that were administered to Muslim applicants only. Baden-Württemberg, for example, queried naturalization applicants, "Shall a woman be allowed to be alone in public or on holiday—what is your opinion on that?" and "If your adult daughter dressed like a German woman, would you prevent her from doing so?" The backlash against the discriminatory tests resulted in federal standardization.

In Switzerland, naturalization continues to be primarily the preserve of cantonal and even municipal governments. Cantons set language requirements and the degree of integration that must be demonstrated (in some cases, this includes a searching inquiry into the social relationships of the prospective applicant). Municipalities get their say on individual applications. Until 2003 some municipalities held referenda on particular applicants; in other words, naturalization cases were decided at the ballot box. This process was effectively nullified when the country's constitutional court required that reasons be given for naturalization denials. But village assemblies continue to have an equivalent, if not final, say. A Dutch-born woman resident in Switzerland since the age of eight was voted down by the village assembly of Gipf-Oberfrick, 144 to 82, for failure to integrate sufficiently because she opposed the local tradition of tying bells around cows' necks (villagers reportedly called her "annoying" for her vegan lifestyle). But the decision was subsequently overruled by cantonal authorities, and the naturalization was ultimately approved.

When can individuals secure citizenship on the basis of ancestry?

As described in chapter 1, children often obtain their parents' citizenship at birth under the practice of *jus sanguinis*. It is increasingly the case that individuals can secure citizenship on the basis of descent on more liberal terms. Emigrant countries have become more expansive in allowing individuals to claim ancestral citizenship after birth, typically without any requirement that the individual reside in the country (or indeed ever set foot in it). Ireland, Italy, Greece, Poland, and other states allow individuals in many cases to claim citizenship on the basis of a grandparent's status as a citizen.

Some countries extend citizenship on the basis of more attenuated descent. In 2011 Hungary provided for streamlined naturalization where an applicant shows facility in the Hungarian language and can provide evidence of Hungarian ancestry, however distant. Residency in Hungary is not a condition for eligibility. Millions were eligible to naturalize under the measure, including large communities in neighboring Romania, Serbia, Slovakia, and Ukraine, in which countries the move triggered fears of nationalist separatism. The move was also controversial within Hungary, where it was seen as a naked play by ultraconservative Viktor Orbán to harness a sympathetic constituency for votes in parliamentary elections.

Is citizenship ever granted on the basis of past persecution?

The Nazi government stripped all Jews of their German citizenship under the Reich's Eleventh Decree of November 1941. Those who lost their citizenship and their descendants are now eligible to have their German citizenship "restored." The extension of citizenship isn't automatic; one has to apply for it. The restoration provision doesn't apply to all refugees from the Nazi regime, only those who directly lost their nationality as a result of the 1941 measure (anyone who had already naturalized in the United States or elsewhere would have lost German citizenship by operation of ordinary law applicable to non-Jews as well).

As dual citizenship gains wider acceptance (the focus of chapter 4), more individuals are claiming German citizenship while retaining their citizenship of origin. Restoration of citizenship isn't predicated on residence. In this respect, the restoration operates in much the same way as ancestral citizenship does for descendants of Irish, Italian, and emigrants from other countries. Eligible descendants of German Jewish refugees in Israel have taken advantage of the opportunity to secure the advantage of an EU passport (which is significant, given the difficulties of traveling on an Israeli one), notwithstanding their lack of any self-identification as "German"—or indeed their repulsion toward it. Descendants of Polish Jews are availing themselves of citizenship in that country under a similar program.

In 2015 Spain offered citizenship to descendants of Sephardic Jews expelled from the country in 1492. Eligibility is restricted to practicing Jews, as certified by the Sephardic rabbinate. Applicants also need to show a "special connection" to Spain, which can be satisfied by proof of knowledge of Ladino, the Jewish language derived from medieval Spanish (a Sephardic cognate to Yiddish), as well as to meet Spanish language and civics requirements for naturalization. Applicants are exempted from any residency requirement. As of early 2018, about sixty-five hundred individuals had acquired Spanish citizenship under the measure. Portugal has adopted a similar measure, with lower hurdles to citizenship, requiring only proof of lineage. Some see restoration of citizenship to Iberian Jews as a somewhat cynical mechanism for attracting "desirable" immigrants, given the failure to restore citizenship to descendants of Moors also expelled from Spain and Portugal in 1492. But the connection of Sephardic Jews to their homeland has remained strong in many cases, even over the centuries, representing a genuine identity credibly supporting the extension of citizenship half a millennium after their departure.

How is citizenship allocated when states break apart?

Citizenship ceases to exist in a state that ceases to exist. The breakup of states—known as "state succession" in international law—poses the risk of statelessness to the extent that former citizens of the prior state are not allocated citizenship in any of the successor entities. The default rule is that individuals should be extended citizenship by the successor state that ends up with jurisdiction over their place of habitual residence, with the possibility to opt out for those who have a basis for affiliating with another successor state. An ethnic tie, for example, or subnational citizenship in a preexisting federal state might qualify for citizenship in a state other than the state of residence.

In the wake of the various dramatic ways in which the maps of Central and Eastern Europe and the Soviet Union have been redrawn in recent decades, the rule has not always worked so well in practice. Some states have appeared willing to exploit independence as an opportunity to exclude those whose citizenship was perceived to be inconsistent with nation-building or otherwise undesirable. In the new Czech Republic, for example, habitual residents with certain criminal histories were made ineligible for citizenship, a bar that fell heavily on Roma residents. In Croatia, those who had not been designated as Croatian by the Yugoslav regime (under a scheme of provincial "republican" citizenship) were subject to onerous naturalization requirements as a condition for securing citizenship in the newly independent state. Similarly, Latvia and Lithuania imposed naturalization requirements on ethnic Russians resident in their territories in the wake of their restored independence. This has created a substantial and persistent stateless community in these countries. In Latvia, more than 250,000 have been formally designated as "noncitizens," afforded rights of residence but denied full political equality. International and regional organizations, most notably the Organization for Security and Co-operation in Europe (OSCE), have pressured these states to relax citizenship requirements for these populations.

Russia has inversely moved to exploit successor citizenship for expansionist ends, playing the co-ethnic citizenship card in the context of its encroachments in Georgia and Ukraine. It has been accused of undertaking a strategy of "passportization," or handing out passports en masse to ethnic Russians and then using the alleged mistreatment of these newly minted citizens as a justification for military incursions (and in the context of Crimea, its annexation). Passportization didn't fool anyone; the international community universally rejected Russia's makeweight citizenship arguments in Georgia and Ukraine. In any case, Russia's aggressive behavior was not contingent on the citizenship status of persons in those former Soviet territories.

What is honorary citizenship?

As the label implies, honorary citizenship is a purely symbolic status. In the United States, eight individuals have been bestowed honorary citizenship by act of Congress: Winston Churchill, Raoul Wallenberg, William Penn and his wife Hannah, Mother Teresa, the Marquis de Lafayette, Casimir Pulaski, and Bernardo de Gálvez (the last three posthumously for service during the Revolutionary War). State Department guidance notes that "such status does not confer any special entry, travel or immigration benefits upon the honoree or the honoree's relatives and dependents." Canada has bestowed honorary citizenship on six individuals, including Nelson

Mandela and the young Pakistani human rights activist Malala Yousafzai. It recently revoked the honorary citizenship it had extended to Aung San Suu Kyi, the Burmese politician once celebrated for her human rights work who has more recently been silent in the face of human rights violations against the country's Rohingya minority.

3

RIGHTS AND OBLIGATIONS OF CITIZENSHIP

What were the rights and obligations of citizenship in the ancient world?

Rights and obligations were deeply inscribed in the citizenship of Greece and Rome. Military service was usually core to one's identity as a citizen. In Sparta, all male citizens gave over the totality of their lives from youth until middle age to the barracks. In Athens and Rome, citizens welcomed the opportunity to serve even though they had to supply their own equipment (which, in the case of cavalry, could be expensive). Taxes were often an obligation distinctive to citizens in ancient polities. Distinguished families prided themselves on their fiscal contributions to public works.

On the other side, the rights of citizenship were substantial. Only citizens could own land, often obtained as a reward for military service. (The right of plunder was a benefit more directly associated with military service.) Only citizens could participate in politics. And perhaps most glaring to contemporary sensibilities, only citizens enjoyed the protection of the laws. St. Paul famously interposed his Roman citizenship against flogging and torture by a Roman centurion, who desisted upon learning of Paul's status. But for his status as a citizen, there would have been no procedural limitations on the official abuse.

Citizenship. Peter J. Spiro, Oxford University Press (2020). © Oxford University Press.
10.1093/actrade/9780190917302.001.0001

In marked contrast to the modern world, citizenship was not a marker of equality; there were many status distinctions, by either law or custom, that elevated some citizens above others. Nor was it an indicator of some sort of national identity—one was either a Roman citizen or not a citizen at all. The ancient world was marked by a range of status categories short of citizenship. Slavery was normalized. One could be a freedman but not a citizen (it was not until 212 C.E. that all free men were extended Roman citizenship throughout the empire). Women were thought incapable of holding the status. Citizenship in the ancient world was hugely valuable to the few who enjoyed the status.

Do noncitizens enjoy civil rights today?

Under international law, individuals have long enjoyed the protection of their own sovereign before other sovereigns. In that respect, foreigners were actually privileged relative to subjects present in their own country. Subjects had no protection against their own sovereign before the mid-twentieth-century advent of international human rights. If a subject were mistreated by his king, he had no one to complain to. A foreigner, by contrast, could turn to his own sovereign by way of remedying a wrong done to him by another ruler.

In constitutional democracies, civil rights were extended to noncitizens by law. In the United States, constitutional protections were extended to noncitizens by the courts in cases involving Chinese immigrants, notwithstanding the prevalent racism targeting them as a group. At the same time that they were discriminated against for immigration purposes, Chinese immigrants were found to enjoy constitutional equal protection; in the 1886 decision in *Yick Wo v. Hopkins*, the US Supreme Court struck down a San Francisco measure that discriminated against Chinese laundries. The Court held that equal protection and other constitutional provisions are "universal in their application, to all persons within the territorial jurisdiction, without regard to any differences of race, of color, or of nationality." The Court later found that noncitizens enjoy all constitutional protections applicable to criminal process. Noncitizens of all descriptions have always had equivalent rights in the face of criminal prosecution. The undocumented immigrant on trial for murder gets the same procedural rights that a native-born citizen does.

This approach is reflected in the international law of human rights. Under the 1966 International Covenant on Civil and Political Rights, a state must extend protections to "all individuals within its territory and subject to its jurisdiction." The preamble of the 1948 American Declaration of the Rights and Duties of Man states that "the essential rights of man are not derived from the fact that he is a national of a certain state, but are based upon attributes of his human personality."

One important exception is in the context of immigration proceedings. In the United States, courts have historically deferred to Congress and the president on the formulation and execution of immigration controls. Although noncitizens facing deportation are entitled to some due process, it is much less exacting than in criminal proceedings. For the government to deport a permanent resident, for example, it need only demonstrate deportability by clear and convincing evidence rather than beyond a reasonable doubt. Unlike in criminal proceedings, noncitizens are not entitled to a jury trial in removal proceedings, nor are they entitled to be represented by a lawyer at government expense.

In economic matters, have noncitizens been discriminated against as a matter of law?

Those lacking citizenship were historically highly disadvantaged when it came to the economy. Under the common law, aliens could not own land or pass their estates to progeny. This was justified on the theory that aliens did not owe allegiance to the sovereign. This common law rule was received into

US law at independence. Many US states barred or restricted landownership and inheritance by noncitizens in some form through the middle of the twentieth century.

Professional and other economic disadvantages were also common. Every state of the Union barred noncitizens from practicing law, and many jurisdictions excluded noncitizens from such other professions as medicine, accountancy, and nursing. Between 1871 and 1976 New York State enacted thirty-eight laws requiring citizenship to engage in occupations ranging from architects, private investigators, physicians, dentists, and pharmacists to embalmers, plumbing inspectors, and blind adult vendors of newspapers. Many states precluded noncitizens from holding a range of licenses, including those related to natural resources, such as hunting and fishing licenses. Noncitizens were legally disabled from operating such regulated establishments as liquor stores, pool halls, and pawn shops. This kind of legal discrimination was sustained by the courts as a rational measure advancing legitimate state objectives. Although much of this discrimination was found in state law, federal law also disadvantaged noncitizens. For instance, many were excluded from homesteading, the frontier practice under which individuals could obtain title to federal lands by improving them.

What were "declarant aliens," and how was the status advantageous?

As a country whose immigrant numbers swelled, the United States could hardly exclude all noncitizens from economic advancement. Many discriminatory measures thus drew the line at those on a path to citizenship and treated them as if they already had the status. It was once the case that prospective naturalization candidates had to declare their intention to naturalize two years prior to filing their applications. These "first papers," as they were known, could be filed after two years' residence (naturalization itself requiring five years' residence in most cases). These so-called declarant aliens were exempted from disabilities that otherwise applied to noncitizens. Declarant aliens could apply for benefits under the federal homesteading measure, for example. A Missouri statute enacted in 1865 provided that aliens "who shall have made a declaration of their intention to become citizens of the United States" would have all rights respecting the ownership of real property "as if they were citizens of the United States."

Exempting declarant aliens from discriminatory measures also reinforced racist aspects of the citizenship regime. As described in chapter 2, Asians and other peoples denominated as neither white nor black were ineligible to naturalize through the mid-twentieth century. Because they were ineligible to naturalize, they were unable to declare an intent to naturalize. As a result, Asians could never qualify as declarant aliens. Some state measures drew the line at "aliens ineligible for American citizenship." California's 1913 Alien Land Law, for example, prohibited all noncitizens who could not naturalize from owning agricultural land. The measure was racially neutral on its face but had the effect (and clear intention) of obstructing Japanese immigrants from engaging in agricultural livelihoods.

Are noncitizen permanent residents discriminated against for economic purposes today?

For the most part, US permanent residents do not face substantial legal disadvantages as a result of their citizenship status. The move away from alienage laws partly resulted from market forces. Frontier states eager to attract immigrant settlers adopted state constitutional measures ensuring nondiscrimination for landholding and related activity.

The courts stepped in where state legislatures failed to scrap discriminatory measures. In 1915 the US Supreme Court struck down an anomalous state law requiring that at least 80 percent of employees of certain businesses hold US citizenship. In

1948 the Court dispatched a California law barring those ineligible for citizenship (read: Japanese immigrants) from holding commercial fishing licenses. As a jurisprudential matter, the key case was the Supreme Court's 1971 decision in *Graham v. Richardson*, which found that state measures discriminating against aliens should be subject to close judicial scrutiny based on the premise that noncitizens cannot avail themselves of the political process. Under that analysis, the Supreme Court has struck down state laws barring noncitizens from law and engineering, as well as blanket civil service bans. In the wake of these decisions, most state restrictions on noncitizen employment and licensing have either been repealed or stand unenforced.

The courts have carved out an exception for some public sector positions for which states can continue to impose a citizenship requirement. "Some state functions are so bound up with the operation of the State as a governmental entity," the Supreme Court observed in its 1979 decision in *Ambach v. Norwick*, "as to permit the exclusion from those functions of all persons who have not become part of the process of self-government." Under this "public function" test, the Court has approved the exclusion of noncitizens from employment as police officers, probation officers, and teachers. But these rulings are permissive only; the law allows states to engage in this discrimination but does not mandate it. Most states, for example, allow noncitizens to teach in public schools, in part as a way to fill curricular needs that would otherwise go unmet. Although it is less common, noncitizens can serve as police officers in some jurisdictions, including Chicago, Cincinnati, and Los Angeles. Employment in the federal civil service remains restricted to citizens, an eligibility criterion to which the courts have deferred.

In the private sector, permanent residents are eligible to work in any profession. Citizenship can only be used by prospective employers as a tiebreaker among equally qualified job candidates; that is, green card holders can only be discriminated against if a citizen applicant has the same qualifications. Notwithstanding near-equality of economic opportunity, social scientists have demonstrated the existence of a "citizenship premium." A 2012 report by the Migration Policy Institute estimated that there is a 5 percent wage bump attributable to naturalization. A study of the French labor market found a 20 percent increase in employment outcomes attributable to naturalization.

While permanent residents or their equivalents enjoy near-equality in the economic sphere, the same cannot be said of non-immigrants and unauthorized immigrants. Non-immigrants are typically admitted for a limited period and in many cases are not authorized to engage in employment. Even those who are employment authorized will often be restricted to working for a particular employer, as is the case with US H1B visa holders. Although undocumented immigrants can sometimes achieve a surprising degree of economic prosperity, they are clearly limited in the scope of their economic activity, which is not legally protected.

Are noncitizens eligible for public benefits such as welfare?

When the US welfare state was put in place in the mid-twentieth century, few federal public benefits were conditioned on citizenship status. Federal courts nullified discrimination in state benefits regimes on the same reasoning they struck down state measures excluding noncitizens from certain occupations. The *Graham* case, in which the Supreme Court adopted a higher level of judicial scrutiny for state alienage classifications, invalidated state laws that limited noncitizens' eligibility for public benefits.

That changed in 1996 with the enactment of federal welfare reform, which made permanent residents ineligible for a variety of federal benefits. Immigrants were excluded from the Medicaid program and federal welfare support (Temporary Assistance for Needy Families, TANF for short) for five years after entry into the United States, and thereafter eligibility was at the states' discretion. They were also excluded in most cases from Supplemental Security Income (SSI) and food stamp programs. Eligibility has since been reinstituted in some cases. For example, all immigrant children are now eligible for food stamps, and all other immigrants are eligible after five years of US residence. States have largely opted for noncitizen eligibility when given the choice. With the exception of SSI, many permanent residents are eligible for most public benefits five years after admission.

Permanent residents are fully eligible to participate in other programs, including Medicare, Affordable Care Act insurance, and Social Security. In other Organisation for Economic Co-operation and Development (OECD) countries, perhaps more so than in the United States, legal residents are eligible for most public benefits.

Temporary and undocumented immigrants, by contrast, are ineligible for most federal social safety net programs in the United States. Some governmental services are delimited on a territorial basis—police and fire protection and munic-ipal infrastructure, for example—without regard to citizenship status. Undocumented immigrants are eligible for emergency medical services, disaster relief, and school lunch programs. Perhaps most important, in its 1982 ruling in *Plyler v. Doe*, the US Supreme Court found undocumented immigrants consti-tutionally entitled to public elementary and secondary educa-tion. In recent years some states have extended other benefits to undocumented immigrants. As of 2017, for example, more than twenty states have made undocumented immigrant residents eligible for in-state tuition at state universities.

Can citizens be deported?

Perhaps the most important right of citizenship is the right not to be deported. This is true under US law, the laws of other coun-tries, and international law. Article 12 of the near-universally adopted 1966 International Covenant on Civil and Political Rights provides, "No one shall be arbitrarily deprived of the right to enter his own country." The body charged with interpreting the covenant has concluded that "there are few, if any, circumstances in which the deprivation of the right to enter one's own country could be reasonable." Banishment and exile are anathema to liberal democracy and the rights of self-governance.

Of course this absolute insulation from deportation is not just a bedrock principle of modern governance. It is also a valuable kind of insurance, affording the citizen locational security in her state of nationality. In a prior era of lax immigration enforcement, locational security may have been worth less. In the United States, noncitizen permanent residents faced very little risk of removal; even undocumented immigrants (those who entered illegally or violated the terms of a non-immigrant admission) had little to fear so long as they stayed out of trouble with the criminal law. With the advent of the Trump administration in 2017, that has changed dramatically. Immigration enforcement has been ramped up in an almost random way. Undocumented immigrants can no longer rest assured that they will be undisturbed in their daily routines. Even permanent residents and other legal immigrants face greater insecurity. A conviction for even a minor crime (especially drug related) can lead to removal of permanent residents, some of whom have been in the United States for decades and/or are veterans of military service. US citizenship thus has real value as an absolute guarantee that one can remain in the country indefinitely.

The insurance value of citizenship may be less dramatic in other countries even as they suffer their own anti-immigrant backlash. European states are aggressive in policing their borders, enabled by natural barriers to entry (such as the Mediterranean Sea). But they tend to be more modulated with respect to interior enforcement against unauthorized immigrants. This is especially true with respect to enforcement against unauthorized immigrants who have long resided in a country. The European Court of Human Rights and other international bodies have interpreted the right not to be expelled from one's "own country" to include those who lack citizenship. The result is a kind of virtual nationality, for immigration purposes, among some who do not hold the formal status.

What other immigration-related benefits attach to citizenship?

In the United States, citizens are able to secure the admission of a broader range of family members than are permanent residents; citizens can petition for admission of parents, siblings, and married children, whereas permanent residents cannot. While this benefit is contingent on family and immigration circumstances, it is often a primary motivation for naturalization.

Citizenship in developed countries also often includes free movement and settlement rights in other countries. Those who hold US passports, for example, enjoy visa-free travel throughout much of the world. Among native-born OECD citizens, it is underappreciated just how valuable a benefit this is; global travel is a much more cumbersome proposition when one has to secure uncertain approvals from destination states months in advance. Citizens of EU member states enjoy not just rights of travel but also rights of settlement; EU citizens can work in any other member state. This "third country" citizenship benefit explains the rising popularity of the investor citizenship programs described in chapter 2. Individuals are not buying citizenship in such countries as St. Kitts, Malta, and Cyprus to live or even visit there. A passport from St. Kitts gets one visa-free travel to Europe, something that even very wealthy citizens of Russia and China do not otherwise enjoy. Maltese citizenship opens the door to working and living in Berlin, Milan, Amsterdam, and elsewhere in the EU.

Are noncitizens required to serve in the military?

Military service has historically been a hallmark of citizenship, the highest obligation required of citizens. In the modern era, many millions of citizens have been obligated to surrender substantial periods of their youth to serve in national militaries, and many millions have died in what is essentially an "ultimate" sacrifice for the community, defined as one's fellow citizens. Also since ancient times, noncitizens have in many cases been able to serve in imperial and then national militaries. As described in chapter 2, military service has supplied a fast track to naturalization.

In the United States, noncitizens have at times been subject to mandatory military conscription. Declarant aliens—immigrants who had taken the first step to naturalization—were subject to conscription during the Civil War and World War I. Other permanent residents were eligible for exemption from conscription, but at a price: those who declined to serve faced a permanent bar to naturalization. Congress repealed the exemption possibility for aliens in 1951. Except as provided by treaty, permanent residents and citizens have since been treated as equivalent for military service requirements. During the Korean and Vietnam conflicts, resident aliens were subject to the draft. Today they are subject to selective service registration requirements. Only non-immigrants are exempted from compulsory military service.

Military service obligations may not be much of an issue for anyone in the future, citizen or not. The nature of warfare and contemporary society are leading states away from compulsory military service. In the United States, there is no chance that the draft will be revived. (There were some calls to reinstitute conscription in the wake of the 9/11 attacks, but they went nowhere.) Many countries have abandoned conscription over the past twenty-five years, among them Germany, Italy, France, Poland, and Spain. Although some states continue to require military service, they tend to be countries that face anomalous security conditions, including Israel, Iran, North and South Korea, and Russia. The trend away from military service as a core obligation of citizenship is clear. In its absence, there isn't much left to the concept of citizenship responsibilities, at least not in the sense of responsibilities that distinctively attach to citizenship status.

Do noncitizens have to pay taxes?

Along with military service, taxes are often thought to comprise a core obligation of citizenship. But most taxes are imposed on a territorial basis regardless of citizenship status. Permanent residents and noncitizens present in the United States for more than half the year are subject to federal income taxes to the same extent as citizens. The only exemptions apply to foreign diplomats and employees of international organizations. Noncitizens are subject to property and sales tax. Even undocumented immigrants are obligated to pay income tax—and many of them do. Citizenship does not result in special tax obligations, at least not for those resident in the territorial United States. In fact, one of the few citizenship differentials in the tax sphere favors citizens; noncitizens cannot claim a spousal exemption from the estate tax.

Other countries also ground their tax regimes in residence. If noncitizens resident in a country were exempted from income taxes, there would be a strong incentive against naturalization.

What are the distinctive obligations of citizenship?

For all the talk of the "obligations of citizenship," jury duty is the only remaining obligation of US citizenship. That is, the only obligation the government extracts from you because you are a citizen is the duty to serve on juries when called.

Can noncitizens vote?

For the most part, voting remains the citizen's preserve; it is the right most closely understood to be a distinctive right of citizenship. But restriction of the franchise to citizens is hardly an inherent feature of citizenship. There is no constitutional bar to noncitizen voting in the United States. States have the power to set voter qualifications within some constitutional parameters (such as women's and black suffrage), but there is no constitutional requirement that citizenship be among those qualifications. Historically, noncitizen voting was widely enabled in the United States. During the nineteenth century and into the twentieth, as many as twenty-two states allowed so-called alien voting, including in federal elections. This was almost necessitated by heavy immigrant concentrations in the Midwest. Noncitizen voting was limited to declarant aliens, those who had started, but not completed, the naturalization process. Noncitizens voted in every presidential election until 1924.

More recently, a handful of jurisdictions in the United States have adopted noncitizen voting in local elections, restricted to permanent residents. There have been efforts to expand noncitizen voting in larger, immigrant-heavy cities such as New York and Boston. In Chicago, undocumented immigrants can vote in local school council elections as long as they have a child in the system. (The same was true in New York before elected school boards were eliminated in 2002.) Other jurisdictions do not impose citizenship criteria for voting in certain special district elections relating, for instance, to water and crop management.

Broader proposals have triggered surprising resistance from progressives, who are concerned that noncitizenship voting will further devalue citizenship as an institution. The logic of noncitizen voting is strong, especially at the local level. Individuals who are subject to state power should have a voice in its exercise. It's a riff on "no taxation without representation." Although voting in national elections might (at least in theory) present conflicts of interest to the extent that noncitizens might look to advance a home-state agenda, this is a difficult argument to make at the local level. Why should a longtime New Yorker have to naturalize as an American in order to have a say over such issues as police protection, subway service, and property tax rates?

Noncitizen voting in local elections is becoming common-place globally. EU member states are required under the 1992 Maastricht Treaty to extend the local franchise to those who relocate from other member states. Many European countries (including Belgium, Spain, and Sweden) allow noncitizen voting in local elections by immigrants from outside the EU as well. Ireland allows citizens of Commonwealth nations to vote in national elections, as does Portugal with respect to citizens of Brazil. New Zealand and Chile allow permanent residents regardless of origin to vote in national as well as local elections. This historical and international practice refutes the conventional wisdom that there is some sort of inherent correlation between citizenship and voting.

As a general matter, noncitizens appear ineligible for national elective office in almost all countries. One notable exception again involves Commonwealth citizens, who, for instance, are eligible to hold elective office in the United Kingdom. Under the US Constitution, only citizens can serve in Congress or as president. (Strangely, the citizenship requirement does not apply to federal judges, but no noncitizen has ever been appointed to the federal bench.) Most US states have adopted citizenship qualifications for officeholders, but one can in theory serve as governor of Vermont or Massachusetts as a noncitizen. There have been some instances in which noncitizens have held local elective office. Under the Maastricht Treaty, EU citizens can stand as candidates in elections in the municipality in which they reside, regardless of national citizenship, and they can represent their country of residence in the European Parliament even if they do not hold citizenship in that country.

Can noncitizens engage in other forms of political activity?

Although voting in national elections remains largely the exclusive reserve of citizens, noncitizens enjoy other channels of political influence. In the United States, green card holders can donate to political campaigns to the same extent as citizens. A proposal to eliminate noncitizen political money failed even in the wake of a Clinton-era scandal in which nonresident Chinese nationals channeled prohibited donations through permanent residents. Most observers agree that money speaks more loudly than an individual vote in contemporary US politics. Permanent residents thus have a kind of quasi-citizenship when it comes to politics. Noncitizens admitted on a temporary basis—even if "temporary" spans many years—can't donate to political campaigns. A 2011 case set up the question on a nonpartisan basis, with claims brought by a pair of nonimmigrant workers—one a doctor, one a lawyer; one wanting to donate to Republicans, the other to Democrats. But a federal appeals court rejected their claim (in an opinion written by now Supreme Court Justice Brett Kavanaugh) that the bar on non-immigrant political giving is inconsistent with First Amendment free-speech rights.

Even noncitizens barred from making campaign donations have other avenues of political participation. Noncitizens are allowed to give to issue-oriented campaigns, focused on referenda, for example. They can hire lobbyists. They can join political parties. They can work as volunteers on political campaigns. That can mean a student knocking on doors or Elton John headlining a fundraiser for Hillary Clinton in 2008. Noncitizens of all descriptions enjoy First Amendment rights. Noncitizens can—and do—speak out about political issues and candidates.

Even undocumented immigrants have political agency. During the 2000s, undocumented immigrants undertook highly visible protests against immigration laws. Particularly sympathetic were demonstrations by so-called Dreamers, noncitizens who entered the United States at an early age. Although these individuals faced little risk of deportation during past administrations, some have remained outspoken even into the Trump administration, during which the danger of immigration enforcement being wielded as political retaliation is hardly non-trivial.

Noncitizens also enjoy virtual forms of representation. They are counted for purposes of congressional apportionment; the Fourteenth Amendment provides that "representatives shall be apportioned among the several States according to their respective numbers, counting the whole number of persons in each State." That is, even though they can't vote, their presence affects how many members of Congress are allocated to each state. Under this approach, California, New York, and Texas get more seats than if only citizens were counted; Indiana, Kentucky, and Mississippi get fewer. The Trump administration has controversially proposed that the 2020 census include a question relating to citizenship status. Even though this would not change the apportionment rule, many are concerned that it would deter noncitizens in general and undocumented immigrants in particular from responding to census surveys, thus depressing counts for apportionment purposes.

Noncitizen interests are advanced by civil society institutions to which they belong. Unions, for example, have morphed from advocating an anti-immigrant agenda to seeing immigrants as a source of growth. The Service Employees International Union (SEIU) has many undocumented members and has been aggressive in promoting noncitizen interests. Finally, noncitizens benefit from the political advocacy of their citizen co-ethnics, enjoying a kind of proxy voice through those in their communities who have the full political rights that come with citizenship.

Do naturalized citizens have the same rights as birthright citizens?

Naturalized citizens generally have the same rights as birthright citizens. It was once the case under US law that naturalized citizens could more easily lose their citizenship if they returned to their country of origin. The Supreme Court found that measure unconstitutional in its 1964 decision in *Schneider v. Rusk*, concluding that the law worked from "the impermissible assumption that naturalized citizens as a class are less reliable and bear less allegiance to this country than do the native born." The 1997 European Convention on Nationality provides that parties "shall be guided by the principle of non-discrimination between its nationals, whether they are nationals by birth or have acquired its nationality subsequently."

In the United States the only disability suffered by naturalized citizens is ineligibility to serve as president; under the Constitution, the office is limited to "natural-born citizens." This constitutional bar followed on the 1704 UK Act of Settlement, under which naturalized subjects were ineligible for the Privy Council, Parliament, and high military and civil offices. Today, many other countries similarly discriminate against naturalized citizens when it comes to national office. Albania, Brazil, Liberia, Mexico, and the Philippines, for example, restrict presidential eligibility to those born with citizenship. Mexico's constitution excludes naturalized citizens from serving on the country's supreme court. In Myanmar, the presidency is restricted to the children of native-born citizens, a kind of double *jus soli* requirement for presidential eligibility.

Do governments help citizens abroad?

As a historical matter, the government's capacity under international law to protect its nationals abroad was among the most important benefits of citizenship. Lacking the protection of home governments, individuals were at the mercy of a hostile world. It was for this reason that Hannah Arendt decried statelessness as a perilous condition in which individuals were deprived of "the right to have rights." By contrast, sovereigns had to tread carefully when it came to the nationals of other states; any injury to a national of a state was considered an injury to the state itself. In the nineteenth century the question of whether a person had nationality or not was often triggered by a request for diplomatic protection. Without nationality, individuals stood alone against the world; with it, they enjoyed the full power of their home countries as a shield. It was not uncommon for states to go to war as a result of the mistreatment of their nationals.

That protection is less important today in the wake of the human rights revolution. Statelessness remains a disfavored condition, but one has the right to have rights as a person, not just as the citizen of another country. To be sure, one remains better positioned in the world at large as the citizen of another state, especially a powerful one. But this is now more a matter of degree than of kind.

States also extend what is known as "consular assistance" to citizens abroad facing various kinds of distress. Mexico has more than fifty consulates in the United States to service the estimated 9 percent of the Mexican population that lives north of the border. These representatives routinely engage local, state, and national officials on issues of general concern to Mexican citizens present in the United States. Under the widely adopted Vienna Convention on Consular Relations, a citizen arrested in another country has the right to contact consular representatives of his state of citizenship located in the country in which he has been detained. That can be an important asset in some high-profile cases. For example, countries whose nationals face the death penalty in the US criminal justice system have mobilized aggressively, retaining high-profile legal assistance for their defense. But in run-of-the-mill cases, consular assistance is usually meaningless. Barring unusual circumstances, US citizens who are prosecuted for ordinary crimes abroad will get little or no help from the US government.

Consular assistance can also be valuable when citizens find themselves in unstable situations abroad. Home governments will sometimes evacuate citizens from conflict zones. Such was the case when Israel battled Hezbollah forces in Lebanon in 2006. The Canadian government flew out more than ten thousand mostly dual citizens at a cost approaching $100 million.

The episode resulted in changes in Canada's *jus sanguinis* rules of citizenship by descent, limiting citizenship to the first generation born outside Canada. The United States, meanwhile, offered a more budget-conscious evacuation: US authorities evacuated US citizens to Cyprus in old landing crafts. The value of this kind of assistance appears to be declining. The United States closed up its embassy in Yemen, leaving thousands of US citizens to fend for themselves in the face of civil war there.

Do citizens abroad carry constitutional rights with them?

Historically, rights applied on a territorial basis only, even for citizens. In the 1891 case *In re Ross*, a US citizen seaman tried for murder before US consular officers claimed a violation of his right to trial by jury under the Fifth and Sixth Amendments. The Supreme Court found those rights inapplicable outside the United States even with respect to a citizen. The Court concluded: "The Constitution can have no operation in another country."

In re Ross was reversed by the Court's 1957 decision in *Reid v. Covert*, which nullified the prosecution abroad of civilian spouses of service members before military tribunals. The Court sustained the spouses' claim that the prosecutions violated their right to jury trial. "When the Government reaches out to punish a citizen who is abroad," the Court found, "the shield which the Bill of Rights and other parts of the Constitution provide to protect his life and liberty should not be stripped away just because he happens to be in another land." The decision coincided with the significant expansion of the US presence abroad, which rendered more practical the portability of citizen rights for purposes of criminal prosecution.

The question of whom the Constitution protects abroad has also been triggered by expanded law enforcement and counterterrorism operations abroad. The 1990 decision in *United States v. Verdugo-Urquidez* found that a noncitizen located outside of the United States who lacked "substantial connections" to the country was not covered by the Fourth Amendment, which protects against "unreasonable searches and seizures" and requires law enforcement to secure search warrants in most cases based on probable cause. But the implication that US citizens enjoy full Fourth Amendment rights when located outside the United States is misleading. Recent federal appeals court cases have found, for example, that the warrant requirement does not apply to US law enforcement activity outside the United States even if US citizens are targeted.

Perhaps the most dramatic example of diluted citizen rights outside US territory involves targeted killing. Inside the United States, the government cannot just decide someone has committed a murder and then execute him; it is the core function of due process to allow a defendant to prove his innocence. Outside the United States a different regime applies. In 2011 a US drone attack in Yemen killed Anwar al-Awlaki, a native-born US citizen implicated in several terror attacks. There was no trial or other transparent process leading to the operation. The Obama administration defended its decision to target al-Awlaki, arguing that the killing of US citizens abroad was constitutional where a capture operation was infeasible and the individual posed "a continued and imminent threat of violence or death" to other Americans. Administration officials asserted that close executive branch scrutiny satisfied any due process requirements; others argued that the drone attack constituted extrajudicial killing. The merits of the al-Awlaki controversy aside, it is clear that the killing of US citizens abroad is taken more seriously than the killing of noncitizens.

Citizenship has proved a marginal benefit in one other counterterrorism context: US citizens cannot be detained at Guantánamo and prosecuted before military tribunals. Yaser Hamdi was captured in Afghanistan in 2002 and transported to Guantánamo as an alleged enemy combatant. Soon afterward it was discovered that he was a US citizen by virtue of his birth in Louisiana while his father worked on a Gulf oil rig. Hamdi himself was unaware of his citizenship, having left the United States in infancy. Hamdi was immediately transferred to a military brig in Virginia. The Supreme Court later determined that he was entitled to some unspecified measure of due process. Proceedings were cut short by his release to Saudi Arabia as part of a deal that included his relinquishment of US citizenship.

Do citizens in US territories have the same rights as those in the fifty states of the United States?

As described in chapter 1, individuals born in US territories have citizenship at birth by statute. However, US citizens living in the territories (including those born in the fifty states and entitled to birth citizenship under the Fourteenth Amendment) are subject to a constitutional differential. Under a series of early twentieth-century cases collectively known as the *Insular Cases*, the Supreme Court found that the Constitution does not "follow the flag" to so-called unincorporated territories, defined as those territories not on a track to statehood. The Court found that the government was constrained only by "fundamental rights," and that such rights did not include trial by jury.

The *Insular Cases* remain good law. As a result, the Constitution applies fully to US government action taken against US citizens beyond US sovereign territory (a proposition set forth in the *Reid v. Covert* decision described previously) but not to US citizens located on sovereign territory beyond the fifty states. The remaining unincorporated territories include Puerto Rico, the U.S. Virgin Islands, and Guam, and at one time also included the Philippines, which did not secure its independence from US administration until 1946. As a practical matter, the *Insular Cases* have effect only at the margins. Most of the Bill of Rights has been incorporated for Puerto Rico and other territories by statute. But US citizens resident in Puerto Rico are not entitled to vote in federal elections even though their voting rights would be protected if they lived in, say, Paris. As a symbolic matter, the legacy of the *Insular Cases* reinforces the differential status of Puerto Rico in the American political imagination, as demonstrated by the aftermath of Hurricane Maria. Territorial citizenship is arguably a kind of second-class citizenship. This discriminatory rule of US territorial governance may now be unique. In 2011 the European Court of Justice found a Dutch rule making citizens resident in Aruba ineligible to vote to be inconsistent with EU law.

Can only citizens commit treason?

Under current US law, only those who "owe allegiance to the United States" can be found guilty of treason if they have levied war against the United States or given aid and comfort to its enemies. In theory, "allegiance" might extend to permanent residents, although it does not appear that any such case has ever been prosecuted. (It would have been appropriately applied to the so-called declarant aliens described above, who had declared their intent to naturalize.) There has been no treason conviction in the United States since 1952, when California-born Tomoya Kawakita was convicted of the offense for his mistreatment of US prisoners of war during World War II. Although many US-born individuals fought for Axis powers, as described in chapter 5 they would have automatically lost their US citizenship upon enlisting in the armed services of a foreign state. Kawakita remained a citizen, and thus exposed to the treason charge, because his conduct was undertaken as the employee of a Japanese corporation. US practice mirrors that of other countries, which have undertaken treason prosecutions against nationals only.

Some criminal laws apply extraterritorially to citizens only. The Foreign Corrupt Practices Act, which criminalizes bribing of foreign officials abroad for purposes of securing business, applies to "US persons," which includes US citizens and permanent residents. In 2003 federal law was amended to criminalize travel abroad by US persons to engage in sex with minors, a criminal measure aimed at the sex tourism trade. Under international law, these measures count as "nationality jurisdiction," under which states can prosecute their citizens for extraterritorial conduct.

Do citizens abroad have to pay taxes?

The United States is the only country in the world that requires citizens resident abroad to pay income taxes. Externally resident US citizens have always been subject to federal income tax requirements. In many cases, resulting tax liabilities were mitigated by tax treaties with most OECD countries, under which citizens abroad are credited for taxes paid into host country coffers. Many external citizens simply ignored the obligation altogether, and enforcement was lax. The obligation extends to green card holders located abroad, who are defined together with citizens as "US persons."

Inconvenience morphed into hardship with the enactment in 2010 of the Foreign Account Tax Compliance Act (FATCA). The law targets the offshore accounts of wealthy US resident taxpayers, but average citizens abroad suffered collateral damage. All foreign accounts held by US citizens regardless of residence are subject to onerous reporting requirements. Foreign financial institutions are also required to report accounts held by US persons, including citizens and green card holders. As a result, many foreign banks refuse to accept deposits from US citizens. The FATCA regime has been especially galling to so-called accidental Americans, those born in the United States but who left in infancy and have never identified as American. Some were unaware of their US citizenship status until they were turned away by local non-US banks. FATCA has resulted in increasing numbers of individuals renouncing their US citizenship.

Do citizens abroad get to vote?

Under the 1986 Uniformed and Overseas Citizens Absentee Voting Act, US citizens resident outside the United States are entitled to vote by absentee ballot in the district of their last place of US residence. There are an estimated seven million US citizens living abroad, a population on par with that of Massachusetts and Virginia. Because they vote in the same channels as other absentee voters (those away on domestic business trips, for example), it is hard to disaggregate their political impact. There is a strong possibility that they decided the presidential election in 2000. The result in Florida may have been tipped by voters permanently resident abroad, including a large contingent of former Floridians in Israel. Notwithstanding their numbers, Americans abroad have not been able to marshal political influence in Washington. Because they do not have discrete representation, their votes tend to get crowded out by other interests. This explains why they were unable to mitigate the harsh effect on external citizens of the 2010 FATCA legislation and their failure to soften the regime as part of the 2017 Trump tax overhaul.

External voting is becoming increasingly common as a global phenomenon. More countries are abandoning residency requirements for the franchise. Some continue to require voters to return home to cast their ballots, as is true under Israeli and Taiwanese law. Others establish polling places at embassies and consulates. A few have enabled voting over the Internet. Some countries continue to disqualify citizens from the franchise after some period of absence. Irish citizens lose the right to vote after eighteen months of external residence; UK citizens lose theirs after an absence of fifteen years.

Although many countries allocate external voters to their last place of residence, a number of states have established separate representation schemes. Beginning in 2001, Italy reserved six upper-house and twelve lower-house seats in the country's parliament for external citizens as part of legislation extending them the right to vote. Of the 4.2 million Italians registered abroad, almost 30 percent voted in 2018 parliamentary elections. Other countries with separate representation for external voters include the Dominican Republic, France, Tunisia, and Colombia.

External voting is sometimes criticized as facilitating irresponsible voting, on the grounds that nonresident voters do not shoulder the consequences of their votes. But external voters have various interests in homeland governance. They may have family, property, and business back home, and will be impacted by tax and immigration policy. To the extent that they do not have an interest in homeland governance, they will not bother to vote. Turnout tends to be much lower among external voters than among resident citizens and is sometimes very low in absolute terms. Fewer than 100,000 Mexicans abroad voted in the 2018 presidential elections there, for example, a small proportion of the more than 11 million who live outside the country. To the extent that external voters have a lower stake in homeland governance, their representation can be adjusted downward. This is an advantage of separate representation, which can be apportioned at a lower level than for resident voters (in other words, it justifies allocating fewer representatives on a proportional basis). Limitations on external voting are more justified when there is a real risk of external voters drowning out resident ones. That explains Ireland's ungenerous policy, given that almost as many Irish citizens live outside the country as in it. But even in Ireland there is pressure from the diaspora to expand the external franchise.

Some political leaders have strategically extended the franchise to citizens abroad with an eye to increasing electoral majorities. Hungarian strongman Viktor Orbán's Fidesz party won an overwhelming 90 percent of the 380,000 votes from Hungarian citizens living in Romania, Serbia, and Slovakia on the way to its April 2018 victory. (The margin was down from 95 percent in 2014, the first time ethnic Hungarians in surrounding states were eligible to vote in national elections after the Orbán government extended them citizenship in 2010.) But such calculations don't always work. Italy's Silvio Berlusconi supported allocating parliamentary seats to Italians abroad in the run-up to the 2006 parliamentary elections. In the end, external voters tipped the balance against the Berlusconi coalition, awarding his opponents four of five seats allocated to Italians abroad and a slim overall majority in the Italian Senate.

4

DUAL CITIZENSHIP

Why did states once abhor dual nationality?

Dual nationality was once considered a threat to morality and to the international order. As the American diplomat George Bancroft remarked in 1849, states should "as soon tolerate a man with two wives as a man with two countries; as soon bear with polygamy as that state of double allegiance which common sense so repudiates that it has not even coined a word to express it." US attorney general Jeremiah Black pronounced that "[n]o government would allow one of its subjects to divide its allegiance between it and another sovereign, for they all know that no man can serve two masters." Theodore Roosevelt later called it a "self-evident absurdity."

In early modernity, dual nationality was framed as an offense to nature, a contradiction to the great chain of being that was thought to order the universe from God to sovereign to subject. In the nineteenth and twentieth centuries it was still reflexively rejected, with bigamy supplying the standard analogy. But behind the social opprobrium associated with the status—which no one rose to defend as legitimate—there lurked much more concrete dangers. States engaged in turf contests over dual nationals that translated into serious bilateral conflict.

European states were loath to concede the loss of military manpower to the United States as immigrant waves moved

Citizenship. Peter J. Spiro, Oxford University Press (2020). © Oxford University Press.
10.1093/actrade/9780190917302.001.0001

westward across the Atlantic. State power was correlated with the number of able-bodied soldiers and seamen. That was the material explanation behind the political theoretic of "perpetual allegiance," under which transfer of nationality was thought to be a philosophical impossibility. European states refused to recognize the legitimacy of naturalization in the United States. For its part, the United States needed new bodies to grow its own military and economic strength, which required admission of immigrants to the citizenry. The result was bilateral contradiction: two states, each of which claimed an individual as its national without recognizing the validity of the competing claim.

Dual nationality was a cause of the War of 1812, as British naval forces abducted from US vessels ("impressed," in the vocabulary of the day) naturalized Americans whom the Crown still considered to be its subjects. More typically, the conflict involved immigrants to the United States who returned to their European homelands for visits only to find themselves locked up for evading military service obligations. This was a particular problem with German states refusing to recognize US naturalization of their native-born subjects. Major diplomatic disputes erupted as these naturalized US citizens turned to US diplomatic authorities to protect them from maltreatment by the homeland sovereigns. In some cases the wrong to US interests was clear. Where immigrants returned home on a permanent basis, resort to US intervention was less justified and in some cases refused. Either way, dual nationals destabilized important bilateral relations, creating serious diplomatic headaches as states staked out competing claims to individuals.

How did states formerly police against dual citizenship?

As states faced increasingly intense disputes triggered by dual nationality, they looked to suppress the status. Abandoning the doctrine of perpetual allegiance, sovereigns not only permitted their subjects to shed nationality but terminated it upon an individual's naturalization in another state. In 1870, for example, the United Kingdom enacted legislation that automatically terminated British nationality when a subject acquired another nationality. Other European states followed suit, either unilaterally or under treaty arrangements concluded with the United States and other Western Hemisphere states. These moves, which played out on a piecemeal basis from the late nineteenth into the twentieth centuries, reduced the dual nationality that would otherwise have arisen when a national of one country naturalized in another. Before the 1870 act, for example, a British subject became a dual national upon naturalization in the United States. After the 1870 act, the nationality was transferred instead of cumulated, with the immigrant losing British nationality upon the acquisition of US citizenship.

That left the problem of dual nationality resulting at birth. The children of immigrants to the United States and other states in the Americas were often born with the nationality of both the country in which they were born and their parents' country of origin (under the former patrilineal orientation of *jus sanguinis*, it was usually the father's country of origin, though in many cases the parents would have shared nationality). This issue was imperfectly addressed through the mechanism of "election." Under this approach, individuals born with two nationalities had to pick one upon reaching adulthood. This was specified by some countries as a formal procedure and by others through informal measurements of attachment. These regimes presumed that the dual national preferred his country of habitual residence unless he took affirmative action to elect the country of nonresidence. Election was less widely adopted by European states, many of which tried to keep at least a nominal hold on nationals born in other realms.

States backstopped election with other domestic law expatriation mechanisms policing against dual nationality. Under US nationality legislation enacted in 1940 and 1952, individuals who served in any foreign military or who served as officials in foreign governments automatically lost their US citizenship. The mere act of voting in a foreign political election resulted in expatriation. For the United States particularly, these expatriation measures substituted for the more awkward election mechanism. Many immigrant children would have had dual citizenship through the interplay of *jus sanguinis* and *jus soli* rules, inheriting their parents' nationality while securing US citizenship through birth on US territory. That was tolerable as long as the other nationality remained dormant. But if the other nationality was activated, US citizenship was forfeited and active dual nationality suppressed.

States could have eliminated the incidence of dual nationality altogether if they had been able to harmonize their nationality practices. For example, in theory, if all states had agreed on *jus soli* birth citizenship only, dual nationality at birth would have been eliminated; all children would then have been born with the nationality of their birthplace only. Likewise, if all states had agreed to cancel their nationality upon acquisition of another nationality, dual citizenship would not have resulted from naturalization.

Serious multilateral efforts were launched to suppress dual nationality. In the 1920s two major blue-ribbon commissions took aim at the problem of dual nationality. One was funded by John D. Rockefeller Jr. and sponsored by Harvard Law School; among its members were soon-to-be Supreme Court justice Benjamin Cardozo, former secretary of state Elihu Root, and two future judges on the World Court. The other was charged by the League of Nations and included top-drawer international jurists. Both laid out specific proposals for the Hague Conference on the Codification of International Law, for which nationality was one of only three subjects under consideration. But the resulting 1930 Hague Convention on Certain Questions Relating to the Conflict of Nationality Laws offered a watered-down response and was undersubscribed in any case. For all the problems triggered by dual nationality, states were unwilling to give up significant discretion over nationality practice.

States also attempted to resolve nationality conflicts on a bilateral basis. The Bancroft treaties comprised a series of bilateral agreements aimed at reducing the incidence of dual nationality. Named after the eminent US diplomat George Bancroft, the treaties adopted mechanisms by which nationality transferred from the homeland to the state of naturalization. The first treaty, concluded with the North German Confederation, provided that a German immigrant would be treated as a US citizen by both countries after five years' residence and naturalization in the United States. The treaty also provided for reversion to German citizenship two years after a naturalized US citizen returned to reside in Germany. The agreement thus addressed circular migration, which was common among immigrants to the United States, many of whom returned home on a permanent basis. The treaty with the North German Confederation was replicated with other German and Scandinavian states, Belgium, and Austria-Hungary, among others.

How does one get dual citizenship at birth?

There are two ways a person can be born with more than one citizenship. First, if a child is born to parents holding different nationalities, the child will often have both citizenships by descent. For example, a child born in Germany to one German citizen parent and one US citizen parent will have both US and German citizenship at birth (as long as the US parent has satisfied US residency requirements prior to the child's birth). Dual citizenship by virtue of mixed nationality parentage and the operation of rules of *jus sanguinis* has become more common as the vast majority of countries now allow citizenship to descend through mothers and fathers, eliminating the formerly prevalent discrimination that rejected matrilineal descent.

It has become more common as a sociological matter as an increasing number of individuals find partners across borders.

Dual citizenship at birth also arises from the interplay of *jus soli* and *jus sanguinis* rules, that is, birth citizenship based on territorial location and birth citizenship based on parentage. When a parent of one nationality has a child in the territory of another state, the child sometimes has the citizenship of both the parent and the state in which she was born. Thus if German parents have a child in the United States, the child will have both German and US citizenship at birth by virtue of Germany's adherence to *jus sanguinis* and the absolute rule of *jus soli* as practiced by the United States. This source of dual citizenship is also increasing as a sociological matter as more individuals live and work outside their states of nationality.

How does one get dual citizenship after birth?

One acquires dual citizenship by naturalizing in a country while retaining citizenship in one's country of origin. This is not necessarily a matter of choice. It requires first that the country of origin allow retention upon naturalization elsewhere. It also requires that the country of naturalization not require termination of original citizenship as a condition of naturalization. In other words, acquiring dual citizenship after birth only works if both countries accept dual citizenship.

This explains why dual citizenship after birth was suppressed with some success from the late nineteenth through the middle of the twentieth century. The majority practice under which birth citizenship would be terminated upon naturalization in another country precluded the status in many country pairings. For example, even though the United States tolerated the holding of other citizenships, on an inactive basis at least, dual nationality could not result if a home state terminated citizenship upon an immigrant's US naturalization. Before 1998 Mexico automatically terminated the Mexican citizenship of individuals naturalizing in the United

States; by operation of Mexican law, then, Mexicans who naturalized as Americans could not keep their Mexican citizenship in the process.

But many states now allow retention of original citizenship upon acquisition of another citizenship. Mexico, for example, changed its law in 1998 to allow Mexicans to keep their citizenship when they naturalize in the United States and elsewhere. That means almost all Mexicans who naturalize as Americans become dual citizens in the process. The same holds true for a growing majority of other states. Even those that purport to terminate citizenship upon naturalization elsewhere for the most part do not follow through on the action, often because they have no mechanism for learning of the acquisition of another citizenship. Few states require naturalization applicants to demonstrate that their original citizenship will terminate upon naturalization.

Is the US renunciation oath enforced?

On the cusp of US citizenship, as part of the oath administered to all naturalization applicants, new citizens undertake to "absolutely and entirely renounce and abjure all allegiance and fidelity to any foreign prince, potentate, state, or sovereignty, of whom or which [they] have heretofore been a subject or citizen." As evident in the archaic phrasing, the oath dates back to the early days of the Republic. On its face the oath appears to require naturalizing Americans to terminate homeland citizenship as a condition of naturalization. Understandably, prospective applicants perceive it that way, and some may even be deterred from naturalizing to the extent that loss of homeland citizenship represents a deal-breaker.

But the oath is not and never has been enforced. In the Republic's early years, it could not be enforced because European states saw nationality as indissoluble (under the "perpetual allegiance" approach described in chapter 1). Thereafter, the United States depended on source countries to suppress dual citizenship, failing which it pursued the hair-trigger expatriation regime described in chapter 5. Taking the oath was also thought to be a kind of sacred showing of loyalty; even if the naturalizing citizen did not or could not formally terminate her homeland nationality, the oath was enough to signify the transfer of loyalty.

Today the renunciation oath is a lamentable anachronism to the extent that many new citizens are forced to engage in a kind of perjury in the very act of becoming citizens, knowing full well that they will retain their prior citizenship. There have been some limp, unsuccessful efforts to enact legislation that would make the maintenance of dual citizenship after naturalization a crime. The better option would be to revise the naturalization oath to omit the renunciation clause. Polarized immigration politics, however, make any initiative to reformulate the oath risky, and the renunciation undertaking, meaningless as it may be, will almost certainly remain a part of the naturalization process.

Why do people want dual citizenship?

Having an additional citizenship can pose benefits, sometimes marginal, sometimes significant, and typically at no cost. As described in chapter 3, citizenship does have its privileges. At the top of the list are the rights to enter and remain in the country of citizenship. In many cases, citizenship in one country attaches to travel and settlement rights in other countries.

For those who have a premium citizenship—from a developed country—having an additional citizenship may not mean much. For example, a French citizen who is eligible for German citizenship (say, through marriage) would not get much in the way of concrete benefits from the additional membership. Within the European Union, the additional citizenship gets one nothing beyond the right to vote in national elections and to hold national office. (It is no coincidence that as the United

Kingdom heads to the EU exit doors, UK nationals living elsewhere in the EU are looking to naturalize in the EU country of residence. Before Brexit, their right to remain in France, Germany, or elsewhere in the EU was guaranteed. After Brexit, those locational rights may no longer apply.) A US citizen who is eligible for Irish citizenship might have some incentive to formalize the tie for educational, employment, or travel purposes, but on average the material advantage will be minimal because US citizenship already promises visa-free travel throughout most of the world.

But for those who hold a less advantaged citizenship, the benefits of dual citizenship can be significant. It can dramatically expand an individual's economic opportunities. In the early 2000s, for example, Argentina and Chile plunged into a financial crisis while economies in the EU remained strong. Many of the hundreds of thousands of Argentines and Chileans eligible through ancestry for Italian and Spanish citizenship were able to take advantage of access to EU economies for employment while there was none at home. Recent empirical work has shown that individuals in Latin America are more likely than North Americans to take advantage of ancestral EU citizenships. The economic differential explains the contrast. Those from troubled economies have significant incentives to exploit the availability of the additional citizenship.

In addition to the material advantages of dual citizenship, there are also sentimental ones. A native-born US citizen who is eligible for Irish citizenship through a grandparent may not expect any concrete benefits from acquiring the additional citizenship, especially if she is not intending to work or study in the European Union. But Irish citizenship may have substantial emotional value to the extent that it formalizes an important part of an individual's identity.

That is a key explanation for why naturalizing citizens are often so keen on retaining their citizenship of origin at the same time that they acquire the citizenship of the country in which they have resettled. In many cases immigrants hope to return to the homeland later in life, and they may continue to hold property or business interests back home; retaining their original citizenship may thus have practical elements. But the sentimental attachment will often also be part of the mix. Immigrants don't want to cut their homeland ties even if there aren't any concrete obstacles to doing so, precisely because it will always be "home." Studies have shown that naturalization in a state of relocation goes up once dual citizenship becomes possible, that is, once an immigrant can acquire citizenship in her adopted country without giving up citizenship in her country of birth.

At the same time that dual citizenship presents psychological and/or material benefits, it typically imposes no costs. As described in chapter 3, there are few remaining obligations that distinctly attach to citizenship. Most obligations that were formerly associated with citizenship are now allocated on the basis of residence. Fewer states have mandatory military service, and those that do typically exempt nonresident citizens. Most important, with the sole exception of the United States, states do not tax citizens resident abroad. In most cases, then, there will be no additional costs to acquiring or maintaining the additional nationality beyond usually trivial application fees. From a rational actor perspective, dual citizenship will be worth it whenever any benefit attaches to the status.

How many people have dual citizenship?

Just as there is no global register of persons, there is no global register of dual citizens. The number of people holding dual citizenship is now clearly in the tens of millions at least. Many countries do not track the incidence of dual nationality among their citizens, the United States notable among them. But the number of US citizens holding another citizenship is clearly substantial. For starters, most naturalizing citizens acquire dual citizenship at the time of naturalization, insofar as almost all retain their citizenship of origin. More than a million Mexicans have naturalized as Americans since that country accepted dual citizenship in 1998. Almost all will have dual citizenship.

Of the top twenty source countries for new US citizens, only two (India and China) refuse to recognize dual citizenship in all cases. Many of the more than twenty million naturalized US citizens hold dual citizenship. Many of their children will also have dual citizenship through the interplay of territorial birthright citizenship and the *jus sanguinis* rules of the parent's country of origin. According to the Census Bureau, about one in four children under the age of eighteen has at least one foreign-born parent. Many will have been born with citizenship in both the United States and their parent's country of origin. Unlike in the past, in almost all cases they will be able to keep both through adulthood.

Some European countries keep statistics on the incidence of dual citizenship. Seventeen percent of Swiss citizens resident in Switzerland hold the status. In the Geneva canton, a whopping 45 percent hold at least one other nationality. In the Netherlands an estimated 1.3 million people have multiple nationality, about 7 percent of the population. In Germany the figure is 4.3 million, or around 6 percent of the population. These are remarkably high numbers given active efforts in both countries to suppress the status. The incidence of dual nationality is clearly growing. In Spain the number of dual nationals increased 500 percent between 2002 and 2014.

How can one be loyal to more than one country?

"Loyalty" figured prominently in the historical discourse that disfavored dual citizenship. Buttressed by the commonly deployed analogy to bigamy, dual nationality was thought to be an abomination insofar as one could not serve two masters. As the world moved away from neo-feudal conceptions of governance, in which subjects served the will of their sovereigns, there nonetheless persisted a sense that dual nationals posed security concerns, that they comprised a kind of fifth column whose allegiance to one state was compromised by allegiance to another. Loyalty to state was considered a primary and exclusive quantity. The social norms against the status were unthinking and reflexive in this respect. It was as if dual nationality simply did not compute.

But the loyalty angle on dual nationality supplied window dressing more than any sort of concrete basis for combating the status. In fact, there were few cases in which dual nationals played the role of spies or saboteurs. This shouldn't have been all that surprising. Spies and others who looked to do damage from within would have been the last persons to want to advertise the competing allegiance. But as previously described, dual nationality did pose a threat to peaceful relations among states, because states fought over dual nationals, each asserting exclusive domain and refusing to recognize the other's claim. Dual nationals were pawns in interstate competition. They did not have significant agency through which to do harm as individuals. The loyalty trope presented a more easily digestible and dramatic rationale in which to root strong social norms against the status, even if it didn't have much basis in fact.

Today the loyalty objection to dual citizenship is flimsy. Competition among nation-states may once have been zero-sum. In that context, there was at least a possible theoretical foundation for the loyalty objection: what was good for one country of nationality would necessarily be bad for the other. But that is hardly a sustainable perspective on interstate relations today. There are few issues on which a win for one state represents a loss for another. On the contrary, global issues are now mostly commons issues, in which coordinated international action results in aggregate gains for all states.

Even to the extent that zero-sum issues continue to exist, dual citizens do not necessarily face conflicts between their states of nationality. Unlike in the past, there is no expectation or ethic that citizens should do the bidding of a country of citizenship. They are freer agents. They may favor the interests of one country or another, but that has nothing to do with citizenship status. Consider the US political tradition of "hyphenated" Americans who pressed homeland agendas even after they were forced to shed nationality in their (or their grandparents') country of origin.

What if two countries in which a person holds citizenship get into a war with each other?

The place of dual nationals in the face of military conflict between their states of nationality poses the loyalty question in its ultimate application. Military conflict implicates zero-sum competition; a gain for one state on the battlefield is inherently a loss for the other. But it doesn't supply much of an argument against dual citizenship. Even in the historical context in which states went to war against one another, dual nationality wasn't a problem. The worst result was that the individual had to pick one or the other. That is what happened during World War II, when thousands of dual US citizens who also had nationality in Germany, Italy, and Japan had to choose sides. This was especially true of males eligible for military service. Any individuals who enlisted in foreign militaries automatically lost their US citizenship, so they were no longer dual nationals when they appeared on the battlefield. This expatriation mechanism eliminated what would otherwise have been thousands of cases of treason, since only citizens can be charged with that crime. But their shared prewar citizenship in the United States did not make them a greater threat if they enlisted in Axis armed forces (or the other way around).

Today, military conflict between states of citizenship is a nonissue. States no longer go to war with one another. Conflict is between states and nonstate actors (or among nonstate actors). Even where undeclared wars pit national armies against one another, dual citizens will almost never face the sort of dilemma that some may have felt in World War II or earlier conflicts. When the United States invaded Iraq in 2002, for example, dual Iraqi American citizens could feel loyal to both the United States and Iraq in seeking to bring down the repressive government of Saddam Hussein. To the extent that loyalties persist in conflict situations, it will be to a people and not blindly to a government.

Conflicting military service obligations—in peacetime as well as war—once posed a significant practical obstacle to maintaining dual citizenship, at least among males eligible for conscription. To the extent that each of two countries required military service, the obligations were either cumulatively burdensome or impossible to satisfy simultaneously. This presented perhaps the most compelling motivation to avoid the status from the individual's perspective. But through the mid-twentieth century many states entered into bilateral agreements to limit military service obligations of dual citizens to their country of habitual residence. In 1963 states of the Council of Europe entered into a convention to reduce military obligations of dual nationals. The risk of duplicative military service diminished even before conscription itself became comparatively rare among states. There are now few state pairings in which an individual will face this formerly heavy burden of dual nationality.

Can dual citizens serve in government positions?

No countries appear to categorically ban dual citizens from government employment. (As described in chapter 3, there are in fact many states in which noncitizens can hold civil service positions.) The laws of a number of states, however, have either statutory or constitutional bars on dual citizens holding elective or other high government office. Among the states that bar dual citizens from holding elective office are Jamaica, Liberia, Bangladesh, and Taiwan.

In 2017 Australia faced a major political crisis when a number of members of parliament were discovered to have dual citizenship and thus were rendered ineligible for the office under article 44 of the country's constitution, which bars anyone "who is under any acknowledgement of allegiance, obedience, or adherence to a foreign power, or is a subject or a citizen of a foreign power." The Australian supreme court found that the prohibition applied to five of the "Citizenship Seven," including parliamentarians who held dual citizenship with New Zealand, Canada, and the United Kingdom. The episode shows the absurdity of the eligibility condition. In none of the cases did those disqualified even know they held citizenship in other countries. Even if they had known, the idea that citizenship in another Commonwealth country should somehow disqualify individuals from office by virtue of putative divided loyalties seems unfounded, to say the least.

Prohibitions in some countries notwithstanding, there are a number of examples of dual citizens holding high national office in others. These include US citizens who have served as the foreign ministers of Armenia and Bosnia and as the chief of the Estonian army. The foreign minister of Georgia also held French citizenship, which she only renounced upon her subsequent election as president of the country. The current finance minister of Ukraine is a citizen of both the United States and Ukraine. Joanna Shields, a dual US-UK citizen and former head of Facebook Europe, served as undersecretary of state for Internet safety and security in David Cameron's Conservative Party government. In 2010–2011 a US citizen served as prime minister of Somalia. One report estimates that 70 percent of Somali parliamentarians are dual citizens.

In the United States dual citizens are not disqualified from holding elective office. Austrian-born Arnold Schwarzenegger, once governor of California, is the most prominent example of a dual citizen officeholder. Although dual citizens are not formally barred from high-level government service, dual citizenship complicates obtaining a security clearance. Federal guidelines continue to assume that dual citizens have a "foreign preference" disqualifying them from security clearances and the hundreds of thousands of jobs in both the public and private sector that require them. This is the only way in which dual citizens are disadvantaged in the US context. The presumption is rooted in a completely anachronistic conception of citizenship in which citizens of other countries are assumed to be doing those states' bidding. Even citizens of friendly states such as France and Japan have been denied security clearance on this basis.

Does dual citizenship undermine the value of citizenship?

While the loyalty critique of dual citizenship is largely unfounded, dual citizenship may nonetheless undermine the strength of the citizen-state bond. Dual citizenship lowers the cost of acquiring or maintaining citizenship insofar as it does not demand exclusivity. That means that individuals will have an incentive to acquire or maintain another citizenship when it comes with any benefit. Where dual citizenship is prohibited, individuals will stick with the citizenship that means the most to them, typically citizenship of the state in which they are habitually resident.

With dual citizenship, individuals can pursue citizenship strategies that are purely instrumental. Becky Hammon and J. R. Holden would never have acquired Russian citizenship to play for Team Russia at the 2008 Beijing Olympics if their US citizenship would have been terminated as a result. Argentines would not activate Italian citizenship if sacrificing their Argentine citizenship were a requirement. Investor citizenship could not exist without dual citizenship, because almost no one would relinquish their "real" citizenship for one that means nothing to them. There are increasing reports of green card holders naturalizing as Americans as part of an exit strategy. As part of retiring to their homelands, they look to ensure that they can return to the United States for visits. The best way to do that is to have citizenship, but only if it's an extra one.

In other words, acceptance of dual citizenship allows individuals to hold citizenship that may not mean much to them, certainly not in the conventional understanding of civic solidarities associated with the institution.

Why have many "sending states" embraced dual citizenship?

During the late twentieth century immigrant-source states of the Global South were almost uniformly intolerant of dual citizenship, more so than receiving states of the Global North. Rejection of dual citizenship resulted in part from cultural understandings of emigration. Those who left developing states were thought to have turned their backs on their homelands. Naturalizing in another state was considered something close to treason; Mexicans at one time widely understood the US naturalization ceremony to involve stomping and spitting on the Mexican flag. Emigrants represented part of the "brain drain" that was thought to keep developing countries from advancing economically.

In many cases this understanding was buttressed by colonial histories and fragile national identities of developing states. Dual citizenship represented a threat to national identity insofar as homeland citizenship in new states (and even some established ones, such as Mexico) might be overwhelmed by citizenship in the states of formerly dominant colonial powers. Security issues presented a parallel concern. Former colonies, often lacking any sense of organic community, looked to detach from their former masters. Prohibiting dual citizenship was a sublimated part of that strategy. Developing countries—immigrant-source states, not destinations—had the ready means to effectively suppress the status. Terminating the citizenship of emigrants upon naturalization in another state took care of most would-be cases of dual citizenship. For example, as long as Mexico terminated the citizenship of its citizens who naturalized in the United States, it was able to prevent dual citizenship in many cases even as the United States came to accept the status.

That situation changed with trade liberalization and transformed understandings of the global economy, along with a parallel shift in self-conception of diaspora states. During the 1980s and 1990s emigrants from developing states came to be seen not as having abandoned the homeland but rather as representing a crucial economic resource. Part of this shift resulted from massive remittance flows that came with growing migrant flows, in many cases representing the largest source of foreign exchange for developing states. Prosperous by comparison to co-nationals back home, emigrants supported not only family members but entire homeland communities. Emigrants banded together to fund public works and other common goods. They morphed from traitors to heroes. At the same time, many immigrant source-states came out of colonial shadows to view themselves as global communities transcending national borders. The very idea of diaspora, which had long been restricted to such ancient ethnic communities as Jews, Armenians, and Chinese, was broadened to include virtually any transnational immigrant identity.

In the face of these shifts, homeland governments came to see dual citizenship as a strategy for cementing homeland ties to emigrant communities for both economic and cultural purposes. To the extent emigrants were permitted to keep the formal tie of homeland citizenship even after naturalizing in their country of resettlement, the thinking ran, the more likely they would be to reinforce a sense of transnational solidarity and to keep sending money home. Retention of citizenship kept the door open for both temporary visits and permanent return. Indeed, where homeland governments were slow to accept dual citizenship, diaspora communities lobbied for it. Starting in the early 1990s, immigrant-source states began to repeal laws terminating citizenship upon naturalization elsewhere. However grudging these moves may have been at first, many states came to not just accept dual citizenship but embrace it. Among states in the Global South that have changed their posture toward dual citizenship are Mexico (1998), Turkey (1981), the Dominican Republic (1994), and the Philippines (2003).

Are there regional variations in the acceptance of dual citizenship?

Though the general trend clearly points to broader acceptance of dual citizenship, the world has not moved in lockstep on the issue. Various historical, cultural, and legal contingencies have shaped national positions on the question. The United Kingdom dropped restrictions on dual nationality in 1948. France and Canada allowed citizens naturalizing abroad to retain nationality in 1973 and 1976, respectively. Constrained by a series of court decisions that limited the government's power to terminate citizenship, the United States moved to completely tolerate the status in 1990. Italy followed suit in 1992.

Some European states have resisted accepting the status. Germany stood out as a state in which many opposed dual citizenship as a matter of principle. For years Germany required naturalization applicants to prove termination of prior citizenship—a renunciation requirement with teeth. But the policy became less sustainable to the extent that it had the effect of excluding German-born Turks and other intergenerational guest worker communities from citizenship. A 1999 law afforded discretion to immigration authorities to allow naturalization applicants to keep their citizenship of origin, as well as to allow native-born Germans to retain German citizenship when they naturalized elsewhere. A 2007 law allowed dual citizenship with EU member states and Switzerland. But those born in Germany with dual citizenship were still forced to choose one or the other by age twenty-three under the so-called option model, a contemporary version of the old election regime. Finally, a 2014 law allowed those born with dual citizenship to retain it into adulthood as long as they reside in Germany for at eight years prior to the age of twenty-one.

Dual citizenship remains a politically contentious issue in Germany—much more of a flashpoint than in the United Kingdom or United States, for example—but it would be difficult to roll back acceptance now that various communities, including Germans abroad, have a vested interest in it.

Other European countries have followed suit, often in response to pressure from native-born citizens who have moved abroad and who want to be able to pass homeland citizenship to their children while they acquire citizenship in their country of resettlement. This was behind Denmark's acceptance of the status in 2014. Norway followed in 2018. In 2010 the Netherlands reinstated a policy of requiring termination of original citizenship upon naturalizing as a Dutch citizen. But a variety of exceptions allow many to keep homeland citizenship, including when a naturalization applicant's country of origin does not permit renunciation. Morocco is an important example in the Dutch context; Moroccans are permitted to naturalize as Dutch even though they cannot shed Moroccan nationality. An estimated 1.2 million Dutch citizens hold dual citizenship (7 percent of the total population) notwithstanding efforts to limit acceptance of the status.

Cultural nationalism in Asia has retarded acceptance of dual citizenship. In China, dual citizenship is illegal as a formal matter, but many Chinese hold two passports; the ban is imperfectly enforced at best. Perhaps more than any other major state, Japan has aggressively policed its prohibition on dual citizenship. When Japanese citizens living abroad apply for passport renewal, consular officials work to determine applicant status in the country of residence. For example, if a longtime Japanese resident in the United States cannot produce a green card or non-immigrant visa, she is assumed to have naturalized, and the passport renewal is rejected. But even Japan is softening its stance toward dual citizenship, at least with respect to those born with the status as a result of mixed nationality parentage, now informally tolerated. (Tennis star Naomi Osaka, a dual US-Japanese citizen, will be an interesting test case. Under current law, she must choose one or the other when she turns twenty-two in 2019.) Other states, including the Philippines and Vietnam, have moved broadly to accept the status, and Pakistan, Sri Lanka, and South Korea now allow it in some circumstances. Although Indonesia continues to bar the status, Indonesians abroad are pressing for acceptance.

India presents a special case. India was among the first countries to tap into its diaspora, launching a series of bond issues specially targeted at "nonresident Indians" during the 1990s. It then established a formal status for diaspora Indians holding other citizenships, "Persons of Indian Origin." More recently, it has adopted the label "Overseas Citizens of India." With the status comes visa-free travel to India, the right to own certain categories of property barred to other non-Indians, and a passport-like identification booklet. But OCI status does not comprise actual citizenship. Overseas Citizens of India, for example, do not have the vote in India. The device circumvents putative constitutional obstacles to recognizing dual citizenship (the relevant constitutional provisions are contested), giving diaspora Indians a sense of belonging without the guarantees of full citizenship. Whether this will satisfy the diaspora community, which commands substantial economic power, remains to be seen. Some have suggested a semi-citizenship like OCI status as a way to reconcile China's opposition to dual citizenship with the growing influence of its own diaspora.

African states have also lagged in accepting dual citizenship. This is among the historical legacies of weak national identities incidental to arbitrary colonial boundary drawing. But there is a clear trend among African states toward greater toleration. Those that have changed their laws since 1995 to soften or eliminate prohibitions on dual citizenship include Angola, Kenya, Ghana, and Rwanda. A 2010 study by Bronwen Manby found that thirty-two of fifty-three African countries allow the status in at least some cases. A database of country practices worldwide shows that only 25 percent of countries continue to terminate citizenship upon naturalization in another country, down from over 60 percent in 1960. Dual citizenship is not yet universally recognized, but there is a clear trend toward broader acceptance.

Why should states allow dual citizenship?

Even if dual citizenship enables low-value citizens (ones who acquire or maintain the status for instrumental reasons), there are strong justifications for state acceptance. Dual citizenship no longer poses significant direct costs in complicating diplomatic relations or creating irresolvable loyalty conflicts. At the same time, many individuals have authentic claims to dual citizenship. One can frame dual citizenship as a matter of freedom of association. Excluding criminal entities, individuals can affiliate with nonstate forms of association as they wish. If a US citizen wants to formally affiliate with the state of Ireland, why shouldn't she be allowed to do so in the same way that she can join the Order of the Hibernians? Should the son or daughter of mixed nationality parentage be forced to choose one parent's nationality over the other's, even though both nationalities will be part of his or her identity composite? As described previously, there used to be compelling reasons to constrain membership in other states because it prompted diplomatic conflict. Now that states no longer engage in turf battles over dual citizens, there is less cause to resist the status.

There is also a political rights argument in favor of allowing dual citizenship. When dual citizenship is barred, sacrificing one's citizenship in one state becomes the price for exercising political rights in another. This argument is most powerful in the immigration context. When an individual resettles in a country, she will over time accumulate interests in self-governance (a period formally reflected in the residency requirements for naturalization). Where dual citizenship is rejected, a price for exercising self-governance and securing political equality in the country of resettlement will be the sacrifice of prior citizenship. But that may be a high price to pay, in sentimental and/or material terms. For example, where dual citizenship is rejected, a Turkish citizen long resident in Germany is required to give up Turkish citizenship to exercise political rights in Germany, even though she continues to have an affective attachment to Turkey and remaining economic and political interests there. In the absence of concrete harm to Germany, requiring effective renunciation of Turkish citizenship seems unwarranted.

Does dual citizenship result in inequality?

Some have criticized dual citizenship as violating equality norms. In some contexts, the argument seems disingenuous. For example, when the argument was deployed in debates in Germany in the 1990s, it was to the effect that dual Turkish German citizens would be privileged relative to mono-citizen ethnic Germans. But ethnic Germans with a single citizenship were as a general matter better off along various socioeconomic dimensions than the would-be dual citizen Turkish Germans. Likewise, when the holder of a premium citizenship holds another citizenship, it will not (again, on average) result in significant disparities in status or opportunity. A US citizen who also holds an EU citizenship will typically not enjoy advantages in any meaningful way relative to a mono-national American.

Some have also argued that dual citizenship gives rise to inequality in terms of global political power, insofar as dual citizens have political rights (often including voting rights) in each of the two countries. This is a double-voting argument, scaled up from the argument one would make against allowing someone to have simultaneous votes in New York and California. This would be a strong critique if there were a world federal government, but of course there isn't. Political power at the global level is projected through more diffuse channels, not only through state actors. Individuals have (or don't have) political power through home governments but also through instruments of civil society, including religions, advocacy groups, and other nonstate identities. The global clout of an additional citizenship will in almost all cases be inconsequential.

The equality argument needs to be taken seriously where a group of citizens of a country whose citizenship is globally undervalued have access to citizenship of a country whose citizenship is premium. For example, the tens of thousands Argentine citizens who were able to acquire Italian or Spanish citizenship on an ancestral basis during the Latin American financial crisis in the early 2000s had a clear advantage over Argentine citizens lacking dual citizenship. As a matter of sociological opportunity, having the extra citizenship in that context creates meaningful inequalities. To the extent that access to the premium citizenship is arbitrary (the basis for eligibility being attenuated blood ties), equality objections are fair game. Ultimately, those objections go to inequalities attached to citizenship as an institution, whether mono or dual. Studies have shown that the citizenship one is born with dramatically affects one's life opportunities.

Can one have more than two citizenships?

With the broadening acceptance of dual citizenship will come an increasing number of individuals who have more than two citizenships. As with dual citizenship, as long as all the states for which an individual is citizenship eligible accept the retention or acquisition of other citizenships, an individual can hold three or more citizenships. As the incidence of those holding three or more citizenships grows, the phenomenon is more appropriately labeled plural citizenship, rather than dual citizenship, though the rise of plural citizenship does not change the nature of the phenomenon.

Plural citizenship will grow more common almost as a natural incident of reproduction. When one parent holding citizenship in two countries has a child with a parent holding citizenship in a third country (or has a child on the territory of a third country with *jus soli* practices), in many cases the child will be born with three citizenships. Over generational time, it may be common for individuals to have four or more citizenships.

Others might look to collect citizenships for instrumental purposes. The rise of investor citizenship (described in chapter 2) will add to the population of plural citizens. As part of the new service of "citizenship planning," global elites not blessed with premium birthright passports (those from Russia, China, and the Middle East, for example) are advised to sequence the acquisition of additional passports. Citizenship in St. Kitts can be secured quickly while one is waiting for Maltese citizenship, which has a longer timeline. St. Kitts citizenship gets one something valuable for the short term, namely visa-free access to the European Union. It's a starter passport. Once the consumer has Maltese citizenship in her portfolio, which features access to the United States as well as settlement rights in the EU, she may not have much use for her St. Kittian membership, but that doesn't mean she will shed it, either. The result may be a slice of transnational elites for whom plural citizenship is part of what makes them that elite.

5

CITIZENSHIP DEPRIVATION AND STATELESSNESS

What terms are used to describe loss of citizenship?

"Expatriation" was the common term used historically to describe loss of citizenship, both when the loss was compelled by a state and when it was voluntary. Expatriation should not be confused with the noun "expatriate," which describes an individual (typically from a developed country) living outside of her state of citizenship, whether or not she retains the citizenship of origin. "Denationalization" is sometimes used to connote deprivation of citizenship against an individual's will. As discussed in this chapter, "denaturalization" applies only to the revocation of citizenship acquired by naturalization. Finally, as also discussed here, "citizenship stripping" has been put to work more recently in the context of efforts in some countries to terminate the citizenship of individuals implicated in terrorist activity.

Why did people want a "right" to expatriate in the nineteenth century?

As described in chapter 1, until the late nineteenth century European states largely hewed to the rule of "perpetual allegiance," a natural law theorem under which subjects born on the territory of a sovereign owed him lifetime allegiance. Under

Citizenship. Peter J. Spiro, Oxford University Press (2020). © Oxford University Press.
10.1093/actrade/9780190917302.001.0001

this approach, termination of nationality on the individual's part was thought to be an impossibility. This regime resulted in various hardships for subjects of European sovereigns who migrated to the United States. A common problem involved naturalized US citizens who returned to their homelands only to find themselves facing criminal sanctions for having evaded military service obligations, as homeland authorities considered them the same as subjects who had never left.

In a more exceptional and more notorious case, several Irish-born naturalized US citizens were charged with treason against the British Crown as part of the so-called Fenian rebellion, engineered by Irish émigrés to the United States. In a criminal trial in 1867, the court refused to recognize the legal effectiveness of their US naturalization, rejecting their request for procedures that could be invoked by foreigners only. The case prompted massive outrage back home in the United States, in Secretary of State William Seward's words, "throughout the whole country, from Portland to Pensacola." The "right to expatriation" became a rallying cry. Several state legislatures and city councils passed resolutions demanding federal legislation to declare a right to shed nationality. As one member of Congress asserted, the right of expatriation "stands upon the same ground as the right of free speech, the right to see, the right to hear, the right to think, the right of locomotion." In the wake of the uproar, Congress enacted the Expatriation Act of 1868, which categorically affirmed expatriation as "a natural and inherent right of all people, indispensable to the enjoyment of the rights of life, liberty, and the pursuit of happiness." The legislation remains a part of US law to this day.

Individuals clearly had a significant stake in this debate, to the extent that perpetual allegiance prevented even temporary visits to their countries of origin. A putative right of expatriation also served US national interests. The country needed immigrants to build national strength, including military strength; having a large proportion of immigrants to whom other states formally laid claim was unacceptable from the US perspective.

The effort was incrementally successful. The United Kingdom relented in 1870, terminating the nationality of British subjects who naturalized elsewhere. (In a sense, expatriation was not a "right" in the sense of an option that could be exercised as a matter of individual choice, but rather an automatic change in status that occurred upon transfer of nationality.) Other European states followed, many through bilateral agreements with the United States governing allocation of nationality to ensure that immigrants had one nationality only. Some states, including Russia and Turkey, refused to recognize the legitimacy of expatriation into the twentieth century. Other states conditioned expatriation on the satisfaction of military service requirements. France, for example, imposed military service obligations even on French citizens born abroad. In 1916 the US government refused to guarantee that a US citizen born to French parents in Louisiana would be insulated from conscription if he were to travel to France—a country in which he had never set foot. (Former president Theodore Roosevelt deplored the US policy as "dangerously close to treason.") Only in 1928 did France step back by removing military service as an obstacle to expatriation.

In the United States, expatriation in the nineteenth century was undertaken as a matter of administrative practice by the Department of State. Individuals who resided abroad and acquired nationality of another state were typically denied the protection of US diplomatic authorities (this in an age when passports were not necessary for international travel). In 1907 Congress passed expatriation legislation providing for the loss of citizenship when an individual naturalized in or took an oath of allegiance to a foreign state. In 1940 these grounds were expanded to include service in the armed forces or government of a foreign state if coupled with nationality in that state.

Did women at one time lose nationality if they married foreign men?

From the mid-nineteenth century through the mid-twentieth century, it was a near-universal practice among countries to terminate the nationality of women who married foreign men. In the United States this was first undertaken through administrative practice, not pursuant to a statute. For example, Nellie Grant, daughter of President Ulysses S. Grant, lost her US citizenship when she married British subject Algernon Sartoris in a White House ceremony in 1874. It was restored to her by an act of Congress after Sartoris's death in 1896. This was representative of nineteenth-century US practice. When a US citizen married a foreign man with whom she resided abroad, her citizenship was lost.

The 1907 Expatriation Act broadened and formalized the practice. The law provided "that any American woman who marries a foreigner shall take the nationality of her husband." That was a circumlocution for deeming her to have lost US citizenship. (It is true that at the time most countries, including the United States, provided for automatic naturalization of foreign women who married US citizen men.) The measure expatriated women who married foreign men even if they continued to reside in the United States. The law was premised on patriarchal conceptions of the family and the supposed impossibility of family units bridging national divides. Expatriation of wives was also seen as a mechanism for suppressing dual nationality. Because the wife in most cases would automatically acquire the nationality of her husband, without the expatriation measure she would become a dual national upon marriage. The 1907 act did provide for the restoration of citizenship upon termination of the marriage; in that respect the law held citizenship in suspense rather than canceling it permanently.

The law played out in lofty circles. Ethel Mackenzie, a prominent San Francisco suffragette, lost her US citizenship when she married the famous Scottish tenor Gordon Mackenzie in 1909, even though she continued to live in San Francisco. (She learned of her expatriation when she attempted to register to vote in 1913 after California extended the franchise to women.) After the US Supreme Court upheld the 1907 law as applied in Mackenzie's case, the women's movement targeted the discriminatory nationality regime. The movement rallied especially after the adoption of the Nineteenth Amendment in 1920, which guaranteed women equal voting rights nationwide. The result of a major lobbying campaign, the 1922 Marital Women's Independent Citizenship Act (also known as the Cable Act) rolled back the expatriation measure. The law comprised only a partial repeal, however. Women who married men "ineligible to citizenship"—that is, those barred from naturalizing because they were Asian—continued to lose their citizenship, as did those who married foreigners and resided in the husband's country of nationality for more than two years.

It wasn't until 1931 that Congress removed these remaining instances of expatriation. The US experience with sex discriminatory expatriation rules mirrored the world's. During the nineteenth century, most countries automatically expatriated women upon marriage to foreigners and automatically naturalized those who married their own nationals. (That did create a kind of symmetry that prevented statelessness.) The issue was only infrequently contested, in part because citizenship and expatriation were typically confronted in the context of military service, to which women were not subjected. But as the struggle for women's rights emerged on the international scene, this discriminatory regime was targeted at the global level.

An attempt to adopt a nondiscrimination clause in the 1930 Hague Convention on Nationality failed, but in 1933 Western Hemisphere states concluded the Montevideo Convention on the Nationality of Women, the sole operative part of which provided that "[t]here shall be no distinction based on sex as regards nationality, in [the parties'] legislation or in their practice." The 1958 Convention on the Nationality of Married

Women required parties to desist from making any automatic changes in the nationality of women upon marriage to noncitizens. That was superseded by the 1979 Convention on the Elimination of Discrimination Against Women, article 9 of which mandates nondiscrimination in the context of nationality laws generally and marriage in particular. Today, no countries appear to automatically strip women of citizenship upon their marrying noncitizens. Many countries continue to terminate citizenship upon naturalization in another state, regardless of motivation; to the extent that women may be more likely to take their husband's nationality voluntarily, nationality laws may continue to discriminate in practice.

What was a Nansen passport?

In the wake of the 1917 Bolshevik Revolution and the end of the Russian Civil War, in 1921 Vladimir Lenin terminated the nationality of 800,000 Russians who had fled the country during the conflict. These stateless individuals were dispersed throughout Eastern and Central Europe. In the era before the establishment of a robust international human rights regime, they lacked any form of international protection. The League of Nations (forerunner to the United Nations) moved to facilitate their resettlement, appointing one-time polar explorer and Norwegian diplomat Fridtjof Nansen to serve as High Commissioner for Russian Refugees. In 1922 the League of Nations began to issue "Nansen passports" to stateless individuals and refugees who were unable to secure national identity papers. Eligibility was soon afterward expanded to include massive numbers of Armenian refugees fleeing Turkish persecution.

Although the Nansen passport did not confer rights of citizenship, it did give holders a form of legal identity and international status. By 1926 more than twenty members of the League of Nations had recognized the document, which protected individuals from deportation and extended re-entry rights. For example, a Nansen passport holder resident in France could visit a relative in Belgium with rights of return to France. The Nansen passport program remained in place until 1942, by which time it was accepted in more than fifty countries and had benefited more than 450,000 individuals. It is the basis for the refugee travel documents that state parties to the 1951 Convention Relating to the Status of Refugees must make available to those qualifying for refugee status.

Can termination of citizenship be used as a penalty for criminal activity?

Banishment was once a remedy for political and certain other offenses. In the ancient world it comprised a mechanism for casting out individuals from the community, both symbolically and concretely. Exile continued to be used by some regimes into the early modern era. In 1915 one commentator observed that it had been "practically abandoned" in the face of developments relating to the theory of the state as grounded in popular sovereignty. Exile also conflicted with the rule of international law that states were obligated to accept the entry of their own nationals, lest they pose a burden on other states (in other words, as a matter of respecting the interests of states, not individuals). Today the consensus is that termination of citizenship cannot be applied as a penal sanction.

The US Supreme Court faced the issue in its 1958 decision in *Trop v. Dulles*, which considered expatriation as a punishment for military desertion during wartime under a law that dated back to the Civil War. In a ringing rhetorical acclamation of citizenship's place in modern society, Chief Justice Earl Warren found that the punishment violated the Constitution's Eighth Amendment prohibition of "cruel and unusual punishment." "Citizenship is not a license that expires upon misbehavior," he observed. Even though the death penalty could survive constitutional scrutiny (then and now), termination of citizenship was something more extreme and intolerable. "There may be involved no physical mistreatment, no primitive torture. There is, instead, the total destruction of the individual's status in organized society," Warren asserted. "It is a form of punishment more primitive than torture, for it destroys for the individual the political existence that was centuries in the development."

Notwithstanding the consensus that citizenship stripping violates international human rights norms, Bahrain has terminated the citizenship of as many as five hundred political dissidents for terrorism-related crimes. As described later in this chapter, other countries have adopted measures expatriating individuals on counterterrorism grounds, but almost all of these laws limit expatriation to persons holding dual nationality. No country appears to expatriate individuals for common criminal activity.

Are there constitutional constraints on the government's power to terminate citizenship under US law?

The Supreme Court has closely scrutinized the government's deprivation of citizenship. Through the middle of the twentieth century, the Court validated the constitutionality of expatriation as long as it was based on a voluntary act. Thus, the Court in 1915 upheld the deprivation of Ethel Mackenzie's citizenship upon her marriage to a foreign man on the theory that the marriage itself was voluntary. The same theory applied to other grounds for expatriation, including naturalization in a foreign state and service in foreign armed forces. Under this rationale, citizenship was restored in particular cases where the action was shown to have been taken under duress. Scores of individuals who lost their citizenship during World War II successfully argued that their service in Axis militaries was compelled and thus on the facts did not satisfy the constitutional test for expatriation.

In the 1958 *Trop* decision, the Court found that deprivation of citizenship could not be used as a criminal penalty. In a decision handed down the same day, however, in *Perez v. Brownell* a divided Court upheld expatriation under the 1940 nationality law for the mere act of voting in a foreign political election. That provision had been adopted in the wake of a 1935 plebiscite in which the Saar was handed back to Germany; several thousand naturalized Americans were said to have participated. Justice Frankfurter upheld the provision as applied to a dual Mexican American citizen who had voted in a Mexican presidential election. The measure had set a hairtrigger threshold for loss of citizenship, including one case involving voting in a Canadian town's referendum on whether to allow the sale of beer and wine. The Court's opinion drew a passionate dissent from Chief Justice Warren. "Citizenship *is* man's basic right," intoned Warren, "for it is nothing less than the right to have rights."

The *Perez* ruling was short lived. In the 1967 decision in *Afroyim v. Rusk*, the Court expressly overruled *Perez*, broadly holding that the government has no constitutional power to take away a person's citizenship without his assent. That pronouncement notwithstanding, the government continued to terminate citizenship where an individual engaged in conduct putatively evidencing a voluntary transfer of allegiance, including naturalizing in another country, even if the person thereafter sought to maintain US citizenship. In 1978 the Court found that expatriation could only be based on an individual's express intent to relinquish citizenship. An individual's citizenship was safe as long as she made clear that she wanted to keep her US citizenship at the same time that she acquired another, for instance by recording that intention contemporaneously in writing. But where an individual took a naturalization oath expressly renouncing US citizenship (such as Mexico's naturalization oath), in the absence of contrary evidence, expatriation continued to result. Even as recently as the late 1980s the Department of State was annually initiating forty-five hundred potential loss of citizenship cases, of which six hundred resulted in involuntary expatriation.

Are individuals deprived of their citizenship against their will under current US practice?

Under current US practice, it is impossible for US citizens to lose their citizenship against their will. In a 1990 policy statement, the Department of State reversed its former presumption that a person's naturalization in another state demonstrated an intent to expatriate. The new policy adopted a uniform administrative standard that US citizens intended to retain their US citizenship when naturalizing in another country. The new policy eliminated the need in most cases to memorialize an intent to retain US citizenship. The State Department in effect gave up the fight against dual citizenship in a 1995 opinion concluding that "[i]t is no longer possible to terminate an American's citizenship without the citizen's cooperation." The standard allows a US citizen to undertake any activity in another polity, including naturalization, without risk of loss of citizenship. The only context in which US authorities will even raise their eyebrows at the retention of citizenship is when a US citizen is poised to become head of state of another country.

Should countries "citizenship strip" terrorists?

In the wake of 9/11 and the rise of the Islamic State of Iraq and Syria (ISIS), there have been increased calls in Western countries to terminate the citizenship of those implicated in terrorist activities. A handful of countries have adopted or revived security-related expatriation measures, including the United Kingdom, Australia, Denmark, and Canada, and they have been proposed elsewhere, including in France and the United States. Except in the UK case, these counterterrorism measures apply only to those who have dual citizenship, to avoid the consequence of statelessness. Some require a conviction for terrorism-related activity, others are based on lesser showings. Most target the so-called foreign fighter phenomenon, in which citizens with immigrant backgrounds have traveled to the Middle East to join ISIS and other terrorist groups.

At one level, these measures seem proportionate to the threat addressed. They are in line with historical grounds for expatriation relating to service in foreign armed services, especially hostile armed services; enlisting in a terrorist group is a good proxy for conflicted loyalty. As a matter of counterterrorism strategy, stripping foreign fighters of citizenship deprives individuals of entry rights, thus denying terrorist groups the possibility of using citizens to undertake domestic terror attacks.

But terrorist citizenship stripping has less utility than meets the eye. To the extent that states are constrained by international regimes against statelessness, it works only against dual nationals. The resulting limitation has drawn fire as unjustifiably discriminating against dual nationals, an argument used successfully in France to scuttle a proposed terrorist expatriation measure there. Some dual nationals will have nationality related to the terrorist activity (e.g., Yemen), but others will have an unrelated second citizenship (in any other Western state), which could create incentives for one country to offload terrorists to another. Those who do join terrorist groups do not formally enlist, which makes the recent measures discontinuous with historical ones.

Finally, the counterterrorism value of citizenship stripping is clearly limited. To strip an individual of citizenship for terrorism-related reasons, a government has to already know of the connection, which means that it will be able to surveil the individual and otherwise prevent the undertaking of terrorist activity. In regimes requiring a conviction, expatriation will be symbolic only, since the target will in almost all cases already be incarcerated (often with a long prison sentence). Those cases based on intelligence or other information sources involve due process concerns. Since citizenship stripping implicates the deprivation of important rights that may be more severe than those implicated by penal sentences, especially rights of residence, it will be problematic to terminate the status on the basis of something less than the strict procedures applied in criminal prosecutions.

In other words, terminating the citizenship of terrorists (alleged or convicted) may not be worth the trouble. That is evidenced by the low number of countries that have enacted counterterrorism expatriation measures. Given the robustness of state counterterrorism efforts, it is surprising that more states have stopped short of adopting terrorist expatriation measures. Those states that have used citizenship termination as a counterterrorism tool have used it sparingly. The United Kingdom appears to have expatriated the largest number of individuals on security-related grounds, approximately eighty since 2006. Australia has expatriated only six individuals since enacting its expatriation measure in 2015. In both the United Kingdom and Australia, citizenship termination has been applied only against nonresident citizens, in many cases those who appear to have permanently relocated abroad in a country of alternative citizenship. Resurrecting an existing law, the Netherlands has terminated the citizenship of four nonresident jihadis. In former times these individuals would have lost citizenship through election and other mechanisms policing against dual citizenship. Citizenship stripping may nonetheless be problematic in application, especially insofar as it is applied in an unsystematic and unconstrained fashion.

Is the United States likely to adopt a terrorist expatriation law?

In recent years there have been several proposals to amend US law to provide for the expatriation of terrorists consistent with constraints imposed by the Supreme Court. In 2010 Senator Joe Lieberman introduced the Terrorist Expatriation Act, which would have added supporting or engaging in hostilities against the United States as a ground for expatriation. The bill was aimed at Anwar al-Awlaki, an American-born cleric and al-Qaeda commander who masterminded the so-called underwear bombing on a Christmas Day 2009 flight bound for Detroit. The rise of ISIS and the foreign fighter phenomenon revived calls for stripping terrorists of their citizenship. Senator Ted Cruz recently sponsored an Expatriate Terrorist Act similar to the Lieberman Act. (During the 2016 campaign, Donald Trump suggested that burning an American flag should result in loss of citizenship, but that would run into First Amendment free-speech obstacles, among others.)

Given the intensity of counterterrorism efforts in the United States, one would have expected these bills to easily be enacted into law. But they show very little prospect of being advanced. That may be in part a consequence of the constitutional jurisprudence of expatriation as elaborated by the Supreme Court. The government cannot use expatriation as a criminal sanction; it can only strip a person of his citizenship when he takes an act with the specific intent to relinquish citizenship. The proposals have reflected that constraint, which makes them much less useful as a counterterrorism tool; the government would have to show that the person not only had engaged in hostilities against the United States but also desired to lose his citizenship in the process. That would be difficult in most cases. Perhaps the only instance evidencing that intent clearly occurred when Oregon-born al-Qaeda spokesman Adam Gadahn shredded his passport on a YouTube video in 2008.

The high constitutional bar to terminating citizenship aside, there also appears to be a sense that citizenship stripping is inappropriate as a counterterrorism tool. The response to the Lieberman and Cruz proposals has been tepid at best, even among counterterrorism hawks. As a practical matter, there is more effective action that can be taken against citizens who take up with hostile terror groups, namely, targeted killing. As described in chapter 3, the government has asserted the legality of drone strikes against US citizens abroad. Al-Awlaki was successfully targeted in a drone strike in Yemen in 2011. Although not specifically targeted in the attack, Adam Gadahn was killed in a drone strike in 2015. Given that the procedural bar for undertaking a targeted killing is lower than the bar for expatriation, enacting a terrorist expatriation law would be nothing more than symbolic.

How is passport revocation similar to citizenship stripping?

Given the difficulties of depriving alleged terrorists of citizenship, it is perhaps not surprising that authorities in Western countries have turned to passport revocation as an alternative counterterrorism tool. Passport revocation is not a form of disguised citizenship stripping in all cases. For example, in the United States individuals can be deprived of their passports for failure to pay child support or back taxes. That does not implicate citizenship; it is more a kind of penalty for failing to conform to certain obligations. (In neither context has the use of passport revocation been tested in court.) Citizens cannot be deported for being in arrears on taxes or child support.

Nor is citizenship in the balance when countries revoke passports to prevent citizens from traveling to conflict zones where they might engage in terrorist activities. In these cases, passport revocation more directly relates to the governmental objective. For example, when the United Kingdom has revoked passports of UK citizens thought to be traveling to Syria to fight with ISIS, the action directly prevents the harm. Beyond losing the capacity to travel internationally, the individual's other rights remain intact as a citizen.

But there have been cases in which passport revocation appears to have been a kind of ersatz expatriation. The United Kingdom has revoked the passports of citizens alleged to be involved in terrorist activities located outside the country, in effect denying them re-entry rights and meaningful benefits of citizenship without formally terminating citizenship status. Beginning in 2013, the United States revoked the passports of a number of Yemeni American dual citizens when they applied for passport renewal or immigration papers for relatives at the US embassy in Sana'a. In most cases no justification was given for the revocation; unlike in the British case, these are not suspected terrorists. The individuals have been unable to challenge the revocations from outside the United States but are blocked from traveling to the United States without their US passports. Since the closure of the US embassy in Yemen in 2015 in response to intensifying civil conflict, these US citizens have been effectively stranded. Although they have not formally lost their US citizenship, they might as well have.

What is denaturalization?

All countries have largely uncontroversial provisions under which the naturalization of individuals who acquired citizenship on a fraudulent basis can be reversed. In its core application, denaturalization applies to an individual who lies about criminal or other activity that would clearly have resulted in the denial of naturalization or prior immigration admission. In the United States the most recent notable denaturalization involved accused Nazi death-camp guard John Demjanjuk. In 1981 Demjanjuk was denaturalized on the grounds that he had lied on a visa application by claiming no participation in Nazi persecutions (a specific ground for exclusion from the United States). As a noncitizen, he was deported to stand trial in Israel for war crimes. His US citizenship was restored after an Israeli conviction was overturned on appeal, but he was denaturalized a second time on the basis of fresh evidence in 2002, following which he was convicted of war crimes in a German court in 2011.

Historically, denaturalization in the United States was put to use in some cases to strip citizenship from naturalized Americans on ideological grounds. From 1795 to this day, the nationality law requires naturalization applicants to demonstrate that they are "attached to the principles of the Constitution of the United States." In some early twentieth-century cases, the government pursued denaturalization of putative political radicals on the grounds that their political ideology showed that they were in fact not attached to constitutional principles at the time of their naturalization and that their naturalization therefore had been fraudulently procured. Anarchists were targeted. The most prominent case was the 1919 denaturalization of Emma Goldman, the "High Priestess of Anarchism," although she was denaturalized on the ground that her husband's naturalization, which hers followed, was based on misrepresentations he had made in his application about his age and length of residence.

Denaturalization remains possible under current US law for naturalization "illegally procured or procured by concealment of a material fact or by willful misrepresentation." In a unanimous 2017 decision, the Supreme Court adopted a strict definition of "material" as a fact that would have affected the government's decision on the original naturalization application. It rejected a broader approach pressed by the government under which the government could revoke a person's naturalization for failure to disclose a speeding ticket. The number of denaturalizations has been low in recent years, reportedly only 130 cases since 1990.

In 2018 the Trump administration established a task force in the Department of Justice to examine naturalization approvals in thousands of cases based on incomplete files. Although denaturalizations are likely to increase, this is an area in which the courts will scrutinize government action closely. The initiative has compounded a general sense of insecurity among immigrants to the United States even though it has resulted in few cases of denaturalization to date.

Are individuals free to renounce their citizenship today?

One can posit an international norm affording individuals a contemporary right of expatriation. Article 15 of the 1948 Universal Declaration of Human Rights provided that an individual cannot be arbitrarily "denied the right to change his nationality." The 1997 European Convention on Nationality obligates states that are parties to the agreement to permit renunciation by those habitually resident abroad. Most states allow nonresident citizens to relinquish citizenship.

To the extent that a contemporary right of expatriation is difficult to document, it is because the right has gone largely untested. For external citizens there is typically no cost to retaining homeland citizenship. With the sole exception of US citizens abroad, nonresident citizens face no tax obligations back home, and among the few states maintaining conscription, almost all exempt nonresidents from military service. At the same time, there are usually some residual benefits to retaining original citizenship. As a result, there is little incentive to relinquish citizenship.

Some states continue to deny or severely restrict the possibility of expatriation, including the North African states of Morocco, Algeria, and Tunisia. These countries as a practical matter are still oriented to the old "perpetual allegiance" approach to birthright citizenship as something one can never lose. The denial of expatriation rights in these countries does not appear to have any downside for citizens subject to the rule. Unlike in the nineteenth century, these countries recognize the fact of dual nationality. By contrast, Iran denies the possibility of renunciation at the same time that it refuses to recognize dual citizenship, even if an Iranian citizen was born outside Iran. Iran treats nonresident dual citizens with suspicion. Several have been arrested on trumped-up espionage-type charges during visits to the country.

There are some contexts in which states can legitimately constrain expatriation. For example, individuals have no right to expatriate by way of avoiding military service, tax obligations, or criminal liabilities after the fact. Most states also condition expatriation on nonresidence; that is, resident citizens in a state are not permitted to relinquish citizenship. In 1998 a federal court denied Alberto Lozada Colon's demand that he be allowed to expatriate while remaining resident in Puerto Rico. Lozada Colon argued that he did not identify as an American (in fact, he saw his US citizenship as incompatible with his identity as a Puerto Rican) and therefore should not be forced to retain US citizenship. As a matter of free association, the argument should hit home: Why should someone who loathes affiliation to the United States be forced to suffer it? The fact that this kind of reasoning has no legal traction shows that the state still has power to impose citizenship on non-consenting individuals, at least when they remain on state territory.

What are the causes of statelessness?

Statelessness is the condition in which an individual lacks formal citizenship in any country. Most cases of statelessness occur at birth. The most common source of statelessness involves a child born in a country in which the child is denied *jus soli* citizenship and is also denied citizenship by virtue of parentage. Statelessness is sometimes the result of falling between the gaps of uncoordinated state citizenship rules.

Statelessness can also result from sex discriminatory citizenship rules. Some countries continue to allow citizenship to descend only through the father. For instance, the child of a Lebanese mother and a non-Lebanese father does not have Lebanese citizenship at birth. Nor does Lebanon provide a *jus soli* basis for citizenship. As a result, if the child is not entitled to the father's citizenship or if the father is stateless, the child born to a Lebanese mother and a non-Lebanese father in Lebanon will be stateless at birth. Marriages between Lebanese women and stateless Palestinian men are common, so the number of stateless children resulting from such unions is non-trivial. Several other Gulf states also deny citizenship to children of citizen mothers married to noncitizen fathers, increasing the risk of stateless offspring.

Statelessness can also result when larger states break up into smaller ones. International institutions have pressed successor states to extend citizenship to all habitual residents, an approach that would in theory allocate citizenship in one of the new states to all individuals who held citizenship in the old state that no longer exists. Thus, in the wake of the dissolution of the Soviet Union, all Soviet citizens could have been given citizenship in the new country in which they then lived. The same holds true for Yugoslavia, Czechoslovakia, and other countries that no longer exist. In practice, however, some individuals come out of the state succession process without citizenship in any successor state.

This is sometimes a sorting problem in the face of internal mobility and ambiguous habitual residence. But typically these problems have been compounded by ethnic divisions underlying state dissolution. Latvia and Estonia denied automatic citizenship to large populations of ethnic Russians who had settled in those countries before they regained independence upon the breakup of the Soviet Union in 1989. In theory they have access to citizenship through naturalization; in practice, strict language requirements have made naturalization difficult for many ethnic Russians. As a result, 12 percent of Latvia's and 6 percent of Estonia's populations are stateless, the vast majority of whom are ethnic Russians. In Latvia they have been extended a formal "noncitizen" status that affords residence rights and a passport, but they are denied the vote, eligibility for public sector employment, and other rights that attach to citizenship only. Regional and international human rights actors have condemned Latvia and Estonia's failure to extend citizenship to habitual residents on an ethnically nondiscriminatory basis.

What are the more notable cases of group statelessness not involving migration?

Statelessness also results from group exclusions from citizenship. Several notable cases in which governments have denied citizenship to native-born populations are attracting increased attention from human rights observers. In Kuwait, more than 100,000 Bidoons lack citizenship even though they can trace an intergenerational presence in the country. Bidoon statelessness is tied to the failure of their forebears to register with national authorities prior to Kuwait's independence from the United Kingdom in 1961. Many, but not all, of the Bidoons are of nomadic Bedouin origin; the two terms are not synonymous. Kuwaiti authorities have persistently denied Bidoon claims to citizenship, in part because Kuwaiti citizenship entitles holders to substantial state benefits. Kuwait is reportedly pursuing a scheme, already adopted by the United Arab Emirates, to buy citizenship from the Comoros Islands on a bulk basis for distribution to Kuwaiti Bidoons. Kuwait intends to assert that the Bidoons would then as a formal matter no longer be stateless, even though the Bidoons have no preexisting connection to the Comoros.

The citizenship status of persons of Haitian descent resident in the Dominican Republic has attracted wide attention. A revised 2010 Dominican constitution denied *jus soli* birth citizenship to the children of unauthorized immigrants and persons "in transit." A 2013 decision of the country's supreme court interpreted the exclusion broadly to revoke the citizenship of an estimated 200,000 persons of Haitian descent born in the Dominican Republic between 1929 and 2010. Most of these individuals had either lost or were not eligible for Haitian citizenship, which had only recently accepted dual citizenship. This development resulted in a large declared population of stateless persons almost entirely correlated to Haitian ethnicity. International actors, including human rights organizations, the Inter-American Commission on Human Rights, and foreign governments, widely protested the move. The DR government responded with a regularization program to restore the citizenship of those whose citizenship was revoked under the 2013 ruling, but the program has been criticized as being incomplete and poorly implemented.

Perhaps the most notorious case relates to the Rohingya, a Bengali-speaking Muslim population long present in Myanmar. The country's 1982 nationality law excluded the

Rohingya from citizenship, even though they had enjoyed equal rights in Burma since the country achieved independence in 1948. An estimated 400,000 individuals are excluded from citizenship by this ineligibility. The denial of citizenship is at the root of the 2017–2018 humanitarian crisis, during which hundreds of thousands of Rohingya fled from the destruction of their homes to neighboring Bangladesh. The government of Myanmar (including formerly celebrated Nobel laureate Aung San Suu Kyi) argues that the Rohingya not only are not entitled to citizenship but are illegal immigrants, their intergenerational establishment in Myanmar notwithstanding. Myanmar leaders have stonewalled any suggestion of extending citizenship to the Rohingya, enabling continued discrimination and harsh governmental policies against the group.

How have states worked to combat statelessness?

Statelessness has long been recognized as a problem requiring an international response. In the early twentieth century it was considered a problem for states more than for individuals, to the extent that statelessness resulted in individuals for whom no state would be accountable and with respect to whom all states would be burdened. A 1930 Hague nationality convention attempted to reduce statelessness in limited cases, for instance by requiring states to extend citizenship to foundlings of unknown parentage on their territory.

In the wake of the humanitarian catastrophes of World War II, states worked more diligently, albeit with mixed success, to combat statelessness. Article 15 of the 1948 UN Universal Declaration of Human Rights affirmed that "everyone has a right to a nationality." The declaration was non-binding and included no operative mechanisms for reducing the incidence of statelessness. The 1951 UN Convention Relating to the Status of Stateless Persons aimed to extend stateless persons a kind of international protection from mistreatment by states in which they were located. It called on states to facilitate naturalization of stateless people, not to reduce statelessness as a status but rather to reduce the perils associated with the status.

The 1961 UN Convention on the Reduction of Statelessness took aim at the status itself. In its lead provision, the convention mandates that parties grant nationality "to a person born in its territory who would otherwise be stateless." However, states are not required to extend citizenship at birth to such persons but rather are permitted to delay the grant of nationality until the person turns eighteen and to condition the grant on a period of habitual residence. Because state parties can also specify that nationality will be granted only upon receipt of an application, many potential beneficiaries fall through the cracks for failure to navigate bureaucratic machineries. The 1961 convention enjoys nothing like the near-universal coverage of other human rights instruments. Fewer than seventy-five states have ratified it. Estimates peg the population of stateless persons globally at more than ten million.

Nonetheless, there is evidence of growing adherence to international norms aimed at reducing statelessness. Of the states that have signed onto the 1961 convention, two-thirds have joined since 2000. Institutional responsibilities for the convention are lodged in the UN High Commissioner for Refugees, which has made statelessness a priority agenda item in recent years, rather than the stepchild to programs relating to refugees that it once was. UNHCR has raised awareness among states and nudged them to make small fixes in nationality laws that have reaped substantial gains. For example, a 2007 amendment to the Brazilian constitution eliminated a requirement that children born abroad to nationals take up residence in Brazil in order to secure nationality, a change made on UNHCR's technical advice that clarified the situation of almost 300,000 Brazilians born abroad. UNHCR has had some success in urging states to abandon sex discriminatory nationality laws that can cause statelessness, including Egypt, Indonesia, and Kenya.

The 1961 convention also prohibits the contracting state from depriving "any person or group of persons of their nationality on racial, ethnic, religious or political grounds." The provision is intended to preclude the kind of denationalization undertaken by the Nazi regime against German Jews. Article 8 provides that state parties "shall not deprive a person of its nationality if such deprivation would render him stateless." This obligation has constrained such signatory states as Canada and France from extending counterterrorist citizenship-stripping measures beyond those holding dual citizenship, since deprivation of citizenship would otherwise result in statelessness.

Are refugee status and statelessness the same?

Refugee status and statelessness are often coupled, but the two categories are not coextensive. Refugees by definition are located outside their country of origin. Many but not all stateless persons are located outside their country of origin. For instance, the Bidoons, Dominicans of Haitian descent, and Rohingya are mostly located in their countries of origin and therefore do not qualify as refugees. Under its formal legal definition under the 1951 UN Refugee Convention, refugees must show that they have a well-founded fear that they would be subject to particularized persecution if they returned to their country of origin. While many stateless people are also subject to persecution, it is not an element of the status, which is defined only by the lack of citizenship in any country.

The two groups have significant overlaps. The thousands of Rohingya now located in Bangladesh qualify as both stateless and refugees, because they have been denied citizenship and are subject to persecution by the government of Myanmar. Excluding 3.5 million Palestinians, whose status is complex, an estimated 1.5 million refugees are also stateless. This explains in part why UNHCR has made statelessness a key agenda item in recent years.

Many more refugees are de facto stateless even though they hold nominal citizenship in home countries in which they no longer reside. Multilateral efforts to combat statelessness have to date almost entirely been directed at the problem of formal statelessness (a stateless person is defined under the 1951 convention as one "who is not considered as a national by any State under the operation of its law"). There are many millions more who are de facto stateless insofar as they lack rights in their state of habitual residence, holding paper citizenship by birth or descent in such states as Syria, Afghanistan, and South Sudan with which they have no continuing connection (or only an antagonistic connection). Just as refugee advocates are turning their attention to statelessness as a condition, statelessness advocates are now turning their sights on this broader problem of individuals who lack a meaningful or protective relationship with any state.

6

INTERROGATING CITIZENSHIP AND ITS ALTERNATIVES

Is citizenship inclusive or exclusive?

In the modern era citizenship has been held out as a foundational element of constitutional democracy. It has been valorized as a marker of inclusion and equality. Citizenship is widely considered an unalloyed good, the kind of thing that one can't get enough of. The inclusionary aspect is evidenced by the political catchphrase "a path to citizenship," as used in US debates about the regularization of undocumented immigrants. In this context, extending citizenship status becomes a tool for perfecting social membership, for bringing individuals fully into the fold. The equality element is perhaps stronger still. Citizenship is synonymous with equality. To posit unequal citizenship is a kind of contradiction in terms. "Second-class citizenship" is a commonly effective swipe at governmental actions or policy proposals precisely because it conjures up the prospect of inequality within the citizenry.

These are obviously laudable meanings. At times, citizenship has reflected and facilitated inclusive community and equality among members. To the extent that citizenship has fallen short of these values within society, either because it was not allocated in an inclusive manner or because it did not guarantee equality, it has supplied a valuable aspiration. Citizenship for black Americans was a key victory of the Civil

Citizenship. Peter J. Spiro, Oxford University Press (2020). © Oxford University Press.
10.1093/actrade/9780190917302.001.0001

War, for example. In succeeding decades, citizenship brought black Americans neither inclusion nor equality, but it laid the groundwork for subsequent gains. In recent history citizenship has been a necessary, if not sufficient, condition for fuller recognition of rights within national communities.

Publics and political theorists alike have processed citizenship accordingly. It has been situated at the heart of democracy. The phrase "democratic citizenship" is a standby of liberal political theory, a bundled good representing rights, equality, status, and agency within constitutional democracy. For politicians, "citizen" is synonymous with "person," practically a pronoun of political discourse. As an honorific form of address, it dates back to ancient Greece. If there were polls for words, it would poll very high.

But citizenship also has an inherently exclusionary element. Leaving putative global citizenship to the side, citizenship in a state is not a universal quantity. Some will have it, some won't. Those who are excluded may be disadvantaged. Some inequalities between citizens and noncitizens are accepted reflexively. We do not reject, at least not on a categorical basis, the second-class nature of noncitizenship. Once it is understood that citizenship is exclusionary, one needs to ask whether criteria for inclusion are justifiable. It is important to apply a critical lens to citizenship qualifications. Much of the material in the preceding chapters can be put to work in advancing critical perspectives. Why should a person born on this side of the border have citizenship while the child born on the other side does not? Why are language tests an acceptable basis for granting—or rejecting—naturalization? Why should noncitizens be excluded from voting? The answers to these and other questions cannot be assumed.

What is the "birthright lottery"?

Among the grounds for pursuing critical perspectives on citizenship is the increasing awareness of citizenship's consequence for life opportunities. Empirical data demonstrate that where one is born (usually coinciding with birth citizenship) is the best predictor of a person's economic trajectory. The child born in Norway with Norwegian citizenship is by that fact alone exceedingly likely (on average) to have a much higher lifetime income than the child born in Bangladesh with Bangladeshi citizenship. This is in part simply a matter of access. The Norwegian already has access to a highly developed economy. She will have access to others as well, through travel and settlement rights throughout the developed world. The Bangladeshi, by contrast, will likely be limited to working in an undeveloped economy in which the possibilities for economic advancement are extremely limited. A smart, ambitious Bangladeshi will have a difficult time securing entry into the United States or EU to take advantage of the vastly greater opportunities in those economies. An unexceptional Norwegian will have ready access to them by virtue of her citizenship alone.

This adds a moral element to a citizenship critique. One's birth citizenship is a matter of luck. No one "earns" birth citizenship. The person born with Norwegian citizenship did nothing to deserve the probability of lifetime prosperity; the person with Bangladeshi citizenship did nothing to deserve a lifetime of poverty. Citizenship sits at the center of global inequality. The question then becomes: Why should some people be blessed by their citizenship while others are cursed? This is a question that only recently has been posed in a serious fashion.

To what extent does citizenship reflect social solidarities?

To the extent that citizenship coincides with community on the ground, its exclusionary aspects and inegalitarian effects might be justified. At least in that case, citizenship allocations are non-arbitrary. If citizenship is mostly a formal way of marking the boundaries of human community, the basis for exclusion will reflect membership on the ground. The fact that the citizenship allocation implicates life opportunities does not necessarily defeat its normativity. Membership in other, non-state communities also implicates life opportunities, and yet we do not deny the capacity of those communities to exclude. Not everyone gets to go to Harvard.

During the modern period, citizenship tended to map out onto community on the ground. Those who share citizenship share more than nationality papers. They had common myths, histories, and cultural understandings. In some countries, community and citizenship overlaid other markers of identity, including religion, ethnicity, and race. (The United States has been exceptional until recent years in this respect.) Community has for the most part literally mapped out onto territory, so that fellow citizens occupied the same territorial space. During the twentieth century citizens faced common security imperatives that came with defending that space.

These solidarities supported robust mutualities. Individuals were willing to share among themselves in ways they would not be willing to share with the world. The political philosopher Michael Walzer invokes the Good Samaritan in describing what duties we owe each other as humans. Individuals have willingly given much more to their fellow citizens. The state has been a powerful location of redistribution, with citizenship often supplying the marker of participation. In the context of security, citizens have given their lives to protect fellow citizens. In the context of resources, taxes have been the mechanism for massive pooling of resources.

Of course citizenship and national community have not always been mobilized toward good ends. The German and Japanese regimes of World War II represented intense displays of national solidarity; they may well have been uplifting among citizens of those countries in terms of mutual support and sacrifice, but they had obvious negative externalities. All wars have been the result of competition among national communities and the position that the interests of one's own country preempted those of other countries.

More recently, citizenship has been accepted uncritically to the extent that it facilitated more attractive exercises in mutual support—social benefit schemes and the like—manifestations of social solidarity that did not so apparently ignore the interests of nonmembers in the way that war did. The state is seen by many as an agent of progressive redistributions. That in part explains the continuing positive valence of citizenship today.

But to the extent that citizenship no longer coincides with social solidarities, those positive associations may dissipate. Human and territorial boundaries are beginning to decouple in the face of global mobilities and frictionless communication. The nature of conflict has also shifted in ways that undermine traditional state-based association. Armed hostilities between countries hardened lines between peoples on an "us versus them" basis. Today's dominant security threat comes from terrorism, which is not defined in national terms. Moreover, the response to terrorism does not demand national mobilizations in the way that modern warfare did. Notably, military conscription is largely anachronistic; though conscription was motivated by security needs, it also had an important socialization function, bringing young men together in an intensive shared experience. Although we very much continue to have security needs, they do not tend to reinscribe national identities.

Will the presidency of Donald Trump and the rise of nationalistic political parties revive citizenship as an institution?

One might suppose that the rise of anti-immigrant nationalist political constituencies in Europe, the United States, and elsewhere would portend a revival in citizenship as an institution. To the extent that these elements revel in a past (mythic as it may be) of cultural, ethnic, and/or religious purity, their recent political successes might return citizenship to its twentieth-century intensities. The nationalists themselves advance a narrative in which the nation-state remains the foundational unit of association. They rally to established national symbology and resist the revision of national canons to reflect demographic and cultural change.

But this surge of nationalism will more likely accelerate the erosion of citizenship as a location of social meaning and governmental action. The nationalist resurgence will further undermine citizenship solidarities. Citizens from opposing political perspectives are finding that they have less in common as citizens. This is another, less familiar framing of extreme political polarization. In the past, citizens might have sustained intensely oppositional political views (take the conflicts in 1968 in Europe or the anti–Vietnam War protests in the United States as examples). But even in the face of severe societal conflict there remained a sense of a shared past and a shared destiny on all sides. Today, that sense of "being in it all together, for better or worse" is not so obviously present.

This can be illuminated by pairing citizen archetypes and the commonalities they do and do not represent. An upper-middle-class, educated American who lives on the East Coast now has more in common with a Londoner who opposed Brexit than with a high-school graduate in Kentucky who voted for Donald Trump. The reverse may also be true: the Trump-supporting Kentuckian might be more comfortable socially engaging with the Leave voter than with his New Yorker co-national. This is also the case at the leadership level; witness the rise of the "nationalist international," the emerging transnational political alliance among the likes of Trump, UK Independence Party leader Nigel Farage, Hungarian prime minister Viktor Orbán, and for that matter Vladimir Putin, who appear at times to be working together against their domestic opponents. Nationalists and globalists (for lack of a better term) no longer even share the same facts, with the consolidation of politically segregated and politically distorted news sources. "Fake news" is becoming a boilerplate denial for characterizations that don't conform with the nationalist worldview.

This is more than the proverbial "tribalism" (another term used to describe polarization); it's as if the two camps are evolving into distinct citizenries in the sense that we have known them. Political opponents morph into the "other" in all the ways that noncitizens were once understood. Trump supporters have been seen wearing T-shirts that read "I'd rather be Russian than a Democrat." That is another way of saying that the domestic co-citizen is the enemy and the foreign national is the friend.

Nationalist electoral successes (Trump and Brexit most notably among them) exacerbate differences within citizenship boundaries and solidarities across them. It is not clear how these divisions within citizenries will be repaired. In the United States, once the Trump presidency ends the New Yorker and the Kentuckian are unlikely to return to the twentieth-century landscape, in which for all their differences they had more in common with each other as citizens than with foreigners. At the same time, competing transnational solidarities are growing in relative intensity. Identity cuts across national lines in a way that irreparably damages the bond that citizenship once represented.

Is citizenship being gamed?

Citizenship is increasingly being gamed. There are a growing number of contexts in which individuals can acquire citizenship strategically. For example, as described in chapter 2, individuals are often able to claim citizenship on the basis of ancestral ties. In some cases the connection is authentic, in the sense that the citizenship is reflected in the individual's identity composite. In other cases the social ties are insubstantial, in the sense that the individual has no real connection to the state of citizenship. Of course there will be a range of motivations, often represented in a single individual.

There are some individuals who are claiming ancestral citizenship for instrumental purposes only. That is, they are taking advantage of the availability of a citizenship for the benefits that come with it, often in the form of travel and settlement rights.

The Argentine citizen who acquires Italian citizenship on the basis of a grandparent's Italian citizenship may genuinely identify as Italian. Or she may just be securing Italian citizenship so she can work in the European Union. Or maybe both. Broadening acceptance of dual citizenship allows individuals to take on an extra citizenship when it promises any benefits, even marginal or inchoate ones (the mere possibility of wanting to work in a country, for example), without having to sacrifice one's primary citizenship in the process. This kind of gaming is becoming widespread, especially in countries (like Argentina) in which large numbers of people are eligible for second citizenships to which significant relative advantages may attach. A kind of social learning process is taking hold. As word of mouth gets around that additional citizenships are advantageous (both socially and legally), more people are availing themselves of the benefits of citizenship shorn of sentimental attachments or "loyalty" tropes.

Investor citizenship more transparently implicates strategic citizenship. As described in chapter 2, more countries are offering citizenship for sale, and more individuals are buying it. An entire industry has sprouted around "citizenship planning" for wealthy individuals saddled with undesirable homeland citizenships, including Russian, Chinese, and other nationalities that do not afford visa-free travel to the EU, United States, and other developed countries. Acquisition of citizenship is purely strategic. There is no pretense that a Russian oligarch purchasing Maltese citizenship, for example, is developing bonds of social attachment to Malta. (Okay, there is a pretense: during a one-year waiting period, purchasers are supposed to develop "genuine links" to Malta, a sop to EU officials who had opposed the scheme.

But genuine links can be established through rental properties, gym membership, and the like; no more than a nominal period of physical presence is required.) Purchasers have no prior ties to Malta; they are not required to learn the country's language, culture, or political structures; and no one expects them to live there. Maltese citizenship is good for one thing, something that has nothing to do with Malta as a national community: access to the EU and other states that afford EU citizens visa-free admission.

Finally, citizenship is literally being gamed in the context of Olympic and other international sporting competitions. National teams are looking to recruit the best players who fit citizenship eligibility criteria. The 2014 US World Cup soccer team, for example, included five dual German American citizens, sons of US service members and German mothers, all of whom grew up in Germany—Americans in name only but with citizenship that makes them eligible to compete for the United States. Teammates also included an Icelander born in the United States while his parents were studying there (he left when he was two) and a Norwegian with an American mother and US citizenship. Players and teams are open to exploiting anomalous citizenship to mutual advantage, teams enlarging their talent pool and athletes getting to play in competitions for which they would otherwise not qualify. (None of the German Americans was good enough for the German team, for example.) Some countries have naturalization provisions allowing for the instant conferral of citizenship for purposes of beefing up lean teams for international competition. Belarus, for example, naturalized US gymnasts Alaina Kwan and Kylie Dickson in the run-up to the 2016 Olympic Games in Rio. Becky Hammon and J. R. Holden played basketball for Russia in the 2008 Beijing Games, made possible by their naturalization as Russian citizens. This is transactional citizenship; there is no pretense that the athletes are acquiring an identity along with the passport.

How is local citizenship determined?

Local citizenship is usually determined on the basis of residence. Freedom of internal movement prevails within most countries, so there are not the same kind of mobility barriers that stand in the way of changing national citizenship. Unlike national citizenship, local citizenship is not bestowed on the basis of birthplace except to the extent that it coincides with residence, nor is it transmitted on the basis of parentage. Nor is there any kind of naturalization process for local citizenship acquired after birth with conditions relating to language, historical knowledge, good moral character, or the other kinds of criteria applied to acquisition of national citizenship. One acquires citizenship in a locality by moving to that locality. In the United States at least, one loses local citizenship by moving away—there is no equivalent, at least not as a formal matter, to nonresident national citizenship. Local citizenship adds *jus domicili* to our models of citizenship acquisition, an alternative to *jus soli* or *jus sanguinis*.

In the United States this rule is enshrined in the Constitution with respect to citizenship in the states; under the Fourteenth Amendment, "all persons born or naturalized in the United States, and subject to the jurisdiction therefore, are citizens of the United States and of the State wherein they reside." In other countries, subnational citizenship may or may not be denominated as such. Rather, local citizenship is often the implied sum of various rights and obligations that come with residence, including notably voting rights and tax obligations.

To what extent does local citizenship represent an alternative to national citizenship?

As citizenship in the nation-state is stressed by globalization, citizenship at the local level may grow in importance. There are inevitable spatial aspects to human activity that demand collective action at the local level, including fire and police protection, primary and secondary education, and the infrastructures of everyday life. While local community may also be diluted by dramatic changes in social interaction—we no longer gather at the general store—there are core aspects of territorial community that are essentially timeless. This is a "back to the future" story. It was once the case that remote national capitals had little pull and that co-nationals in varying quadrants had little in common, to the point that they could hardly understand each other. Modernity consolidated citizenries as "imagined communities" of kinship despite the lack of face-to-face interaction.

Although the communications revolution has diluted the significance of distance, the primary casualty may be national identity rather than local identity. As the rest of the world is less differentiated, nation to nation, many people are returning to their localities as a more important site of identity and membership. Notwithstanding the ease with which local citizenship is acquired, local identities in many cases are flourishing. This has important governance implications. With strengthening local solidarities comes a renewed trust in local government. In the United States, at the same time that national politics suffers severe pathologies, local institutions in many jurisdictions are enjoying a renaissance. The phenomenon is virtuously self-reinforcing. To the extent that subnational governance enjoys success, local citizens become more invested in the subnational identity. Because local citizenship is so easily established within nations, competitive pressures tend to boost other factors that intensify local identities. To the extent that local institutions fail, individuals can vote with their feet in a way that is encumbered at the level of the nation-state.

In the United States, can states discriminate against citizens of other states?

State citizenship has little formal consequence in the US constitutional scheme. Using various constitutional tools, including the Constitution's "privileges and immunities" clause, the right to travel, and the interstate commerce clause, the US Supreme Court has severely limited the ways in which states can discriminate against citizens of other states. Most of the cases have involved states discriminating against newcomers from other states. For example, in *Dunn v. Blumstein* the Supreme Court struck down a Tennessee law denying the vote to new residents during their first year of residence. In *Saenz v. Roe* the court struck down a California law capping welfare benefits for new residents at the level that they had been receiving in their last state of residence (other states being less generous than California).

There are two contexts in which states (and localities) can discriminate against citizens of other states (or other localities). States and localities may discriminate against outsiders with respect to natural and recreational resources. For example, states can charge out-of-state residents more for hunting licenses and the like, and localities can charge nonresidents more for beach access and golf courses. The tax burden shouldered by local residents in maintaining the facilities justifies the differential. More significantly, states have also been allowed to discriminate against citizens of other states with respect to college tuition. Again, the rationale is that states should be able to husband their fiscal resources for their own, on the (perhaps dubious) premise that in-state residents will be more likely to stay in the state after graduation, engaging in productive economic activity through which states can recoup the education subsidy.

Can local and national citizenship be decoupled?

Local citizenship is nested in national citizenship. That is, one can only have formal citizenship in a subnational jurisdiction when one has citizenship in the nation of which it is a part. One can only be a citizen of the state of New York if one is a citizen of the United States.

But there is no inherent reason for local citizenship to be conditioned on national citizenship. At a conceptual level, it is easy to think of cases in which an individual is a member of a local community but not the national one of which it is a part. A longtime resident of Berlin might feel very much a Berliner but not a German, for example. Some elements of local citizenship are already being decoupled from national citizenship. As described in chapter 3, noncitizen voting at the local level is increasingly common worldwide, comprising a kind of local citizenship for noncitizens. In the United States, state citizenship has conventionally been thought conditional on national citizenship. But there would be no constitutional bar to decoupling state from national citizenship. (Ironically, the proposition is supported by the Supreme Court's infamous *Dred Scott* decision, denying national citizenship to blacks while finding them capable of holding state citizenship.) New York state has considered extending formal state citizenship to non-U.S. citizens regardless of immigration status, though the move would be of expressive value only.

Can one have "dual" local citizenship?

At the same time that dual citizenship among nations is increasingly accepted, dual local citizenship strangely presents a challenge. Whereas any political inequalities caused by national dual citizenship are attenuated, dual local citizenship within the confines of the nation-state creates more direct issues of political inequality. If a citizen gets to vote within two jurisdictions within a nation-state, she will arguably have twice the political power as the fellow citizen voting in only one jurisdiction. This double-voting problem would be particularly apparent if a citizen had more than one vote for national representatives, say, having votes in two jurisdictions for members of the same parliament. But there appears to be an aversion to double voting even in local elections.

This fails to address serious issues in local accountability. More so than at the global level, individuals increasingly sustain interests and identities across local jurisdictional boundaries. A person can live in one jurisdiction, work in another, have another property in a third, and pay taxes in all three. And yet that person is allowed to vote in only one of those jurisdictions even though she clearly has self-governance interests in each. In 2002 two New Yorkers challenged the state's refusal to allow them to register to vote in both New York City and the Hamptons towns in which they also owned houses. A federal appeals court rejected the suit, acknowledging that they had substantial interests in both jurisdictions but denying the possibility of a workable standard for apportioning votes in such cases. Although rich summer-home owners hardly make the most sympathetic plaintiffs, it is nonetheless the case that they have been dispossessed of voting rights in locales in which they have a clear stake at the same time that allowing them the additional vote would raise not only workability but also inequality objections.

Harvard law scholar Gerald Frug suggests that all citizens be allocated multiple votes, which they could then use in any jurisdiction, including using all votes in a single jurisdiction. Although the scheme would have workability problems of its own and would invite strategic voting at a new, more intricate level, it highlights the contradictions of the current system and the rejection of multiple local citizenships.

What is the significance of European Union citizenship?

All citizens of the twenty-eight member states of the European Union also hold EU citizenship. Under the 1992 Maastricht Treaty, EU citizens can live and work in any EU member state. As a general matter, member states must treat EU citizens from other member states in the same way that they treat their own citizens. EU citizens resident in other EU member states are entitled to vote and run for office in local and EU parliamentary elections in their place of residence, even though they lack citizenship in that country. EU citizenship is not by any means as thick as US citizenship—member states can restrict movement motivated to secure better public benefits, for example, and there remain deep cultural, political, and socioeconomic divisions that retard a sense of shared European identity—but EU citizenship has emerged as a meaningful institution for the individuals who hold it.

EU citizenship is entirely parasitic on member state nationality rules. There are no rules of birthright EU citizenship or naturalization rules for acquiring EU citizenship; the only way to acquire EU citizenship is by acquiring citizenship in a member state by operation of its own citizenship laws. The European Court of Justice has found that the EU must respect member state nationality rules, including where a member state allows dual nationality and extends citizenship on the basis of descent. This is why EU citizenship is so valuable (literally, in the case of Malta's and Cyprus's "citizenship for sale" programs). It doesn't matter how one secures the national citizenship that results in the possession of EU citizenship; once one has it, it cannot be second-guessed by another member state.

Because it is contingent on member state citizenship, what can be gained can also be lost. This is true at the individual level; if one renounces one's citizenship in an EU member state, EU citizenship is also forfeited. This will almost surely be the case at the collective level as well. If the United Kingdom exits the European Union, all UK citizens will also forfeit their EU citizenship unless they hold citizenship in another EU member state. Applications by UK citizens for other member state citizenship have spiked since the 2016 Brexit referendum vote. Some are eligible as longtime residents of other member states. In the past they have had no real reason to naturalize in their place of residence, since EU citizenship guaranteed them the right to work and live elsewhere in the EU; now their residence outside the United Kingdom may depend on acquiring the other citizenship. There has also been a dramatic increase in

UK citizen applications for Irish citizenship, which shows no signs of leaving the EU. As many as six million UK citizens are eligible for Irish citizenship either by descent or by birth anywhere on the island of Ireland (including Northern Ireland). Many are likely to secure Irish citizenship in the wake of Brexit by way of retaining free movement rights on the continent, another significant example of strategic citizenship acquisition.

How does citizenship relate to "good citizenship"?

As a descriptor, "citizenship" is not always or even mostly used to denote the formal status of citizenship. In loose political talk, "citizen" is deployed as a respectful form of address that really means "you people listening to my speech," whether or not everyone in an audience actually has citizenship. A politician giving a university graduation address, for example, might use the term even though there are many noncitizen international students in attendance.

Perhaps even more so, "good citizen" has been untethered from the legal status of citizenship. A person can be a good citizen without being a citizen. People might argue over what exactly constitutes good citizenship, but most would agree that it can be achieved through various forms of civic activity, for example, volunteering for a charity, being active in a child's school, or working with a neighborhood association. Of course political participation, voting included, presents one route to good citizenship that might be at least partially blocked to the noncitizen. But no one would question an individual's informal entitlement to good citizenship status on the grounds that she lacked citizenship status. In this context, "citizenship" has taken on a metaphorical quality.

Can citizenship translate to other forms of community?

Citizenship is formally a creature only of the state, institutionalizing membership in the state. But citizenship practices may inform membership practices in other communities. Religious communities supply interesting parallels. Religions largely adhere to *jus sanguinis* practices, to the extent that many are born into the religion of their parents. Unlike citizenship in the state, many religions have a coming-of-age process by which the young adult acquires community principles and history and membership is confirmed, such as the bar and bat mitzvahs of Judaism. Almost all religions provide for conversion, which resembles naturalization in the state.

Many religions also have rules for expulsion from the religious community (for example, excommunication from the Catholic Church), which parallels expatriation. Benefits accrue to members of the religion only, in a way similar to the advantaging of citizens over noncitizens, beginning with salvation. Obligations are specified and can intrude into everyday conduct. Some religions have their own form of tax, such as the tithe in Christianity. Compliance with tithing in the Mormon Church has been shown to be higher than compliance with US federal tax obligations.

Religions present particularly close parallels because they have long histories and once loomed as communities more important than states. But all communities have membership rules, formal and informal, which state citizenship practices can illuminate. Generally, the stronger the community, the higher the barriers to admission. It's easy to join a political party, for example, but membership alone doesn't get you much. Some communities are oriented to immutable forms of identity, such as sexual orientation, ethnicity, and race, but even these have membership issues at the margins. Native American and other indigenous tribes supply interesting membership questions, in many cases literally measured by blood quantum.

Membership rules in nonstate communities can also be normatively informed by citizenship practice. As with citizenship admission, nonstate communities discriminate with respect to membership. You can't be a Catholic if your professed beliefs conflict with the church teachings. It couldn't be any other way.

But if the Catholic Church were to deny membership on the basis of race, other questions would be raised. Nonstate communities are allowed a large measure of self-determination. That may be why some appear to be eclipsing state-based community. But nonstate communities should not be exempted from fairness and justice values in their membership practices.

Is "global citizenship" a meaningful aspiration?

"Global citizenship" is often derided by nationalists. "If you believe you are a citizen of the world," British prime minister Theresa May has said, "you are a citizen of nowhere. You don't understand what citizenship means." In response to "a lot of talk about how we are becoming a 'globalized world,'" Donald Trump blares, "there is no global anthem. No global currency. No certificate of global citizenship. We pledge allegiance to one flag and that flag is the American flag."

They have a point. At one level, citizenship inherently implicates difference. Citizenship as we have known it has always involved boundaries drawn between insiders and outsiders; indeed, much of this book has been devoted to how those boundaries are delineated. To say that all of humanity can share a single global citizenship is something of a contradiction in terms. (It would only make sense relative to extraterrestrials.) This is especially true insofar as global citizenship is associated with the end of conflict and a sort of deracination of humanity. There will always be distinct communities of state or nonstate definition dividing humanity into sometimes competitive subgroups.

Global citizenship is only somewhat more plausible when framed in terms of world federation. This concept dates back at least to the eighteenth-century philosopher Immanuel Kant, who saw a "perpetual peace" in a federation of free states. The concept was revived in the wake of the two world wars and the establishment of the United Nations (the World Federalist Movement was chartered as a nongovernmental organization in 1947) but quickly fell victim to the Cold War, which made visions of world government seem far-fetched. More recently, the end of the Cold War saw some advancing blueprints for global government. World federalism seeks in effect to establish a global parliament. Most proposals (Kant's included) use nation-states as building blocks in the way that the United States uses states and the European Union uses member states. These are realistic ideas in the sense of working with meaningful sociological units. But they ignore the attenuations of representative democracy. Legislators are too distant already in national capitals. Using the ballot box to keep representatives accountable at the global level seems impractical, and the global citizenship of world federalism has failed to catch on.

There is one sense in which global citizenship may be meaningful. With the rise of the human rights culture, there appears to be some near-universal understanding that humanity comprises a community to the extent that human beings are understood to have dignity and to deserve protection from some forms of cruelty. The margins may be unclear, but no actor accepted as legitimate by the world community would, for example, openly engage in torture denominated as such. To the extent that humanity shares certain values, a kind of community exists around it. This global community and the global citizenship that goes with it will never be of a piece with national community or national citizenship. Global citizenship is inclusive to the extent that everyone will have it, but it will always be supplementary to other forms of citizenship, state and nonstate.

BIBLIOGRAPHIC NOTE

There are a number of good resources for those looking for further information on the subject of citizenship. *The Oxford Handbook of Citizenship* (Oxford University Press 2018) provides an excellent conceptual framing of the subject, with thirty-seven entries from leading scholars from a range of academic disciplines. For those looking for information on particular countries, the European University Institute's Globalcit database (globalcit.eu) maintains a systematized clearinghouse of state citizenship practices. EUI has also issued excellent country reports on many of the world's states. Valuable earlier projects analyzing citizenship in comparative perspective include multivolume studies from the Carnegie Endowment for International Peace, led by T. Alexander Aleinikoff, and the EU research project on International Migration, Integration, and Social Cohesion (IMISCOE), led by Rainer Bauböck.

As citizenship has presented more urgent issues in the wake of increased migration flows and contested national identities, several books focus on specific countries and regions. Among them are Bronwen Manby, *Citizenship Laws in Africa: A Comparative Study* (Open Society 2010); Diego Acosta, *The National Versus the Foreigner in Latin America* (Cambridge University Press 2018); Erin Aeran Chung, *Immigration and Citizenship in Japan* (Cambridge University Press 2010); Nils A. Butenschøn et al., *Citizenship and the State in the Middle East* (Syracuse University Press 2000); and Marc Morjé Howard, *The Politics of Citizenship in Europe* (Cambridge University Press 2009). Kamal Sadiq takes an interesting look at citizenship in the Global South in *Paper Citizens: How Illegal Immigrants Acquire Citizenship in Developing Countries* (Oxford University Press 2010). On the history of French citizenship, Patrick Weil's *How to Be French: Nationality in the Making since 1789* (Duke University Press 2008) is definitive. My book *Beyond Citizenship: American Identity After Globalization* (Oxford University Press 2008) situates US citizenship practice in historical, legal, and theoretical contexts. Rogers M. Smith's magisterial *Civic Ideals: Conflicting Visions of Citizenship in U.S. History* (Yale University Press 1997) recounts the long arc of US citizenship, warts and all. For an argument for reinforcing US citizenship on restrictive terms, see Samuel P. Huntington's *Who Are We? The Challenges to America's National Identity* (Simon & Schuster 2005).

Some contemporaneous historical work adds an interesting perspective while showing how important nationality has sometimes loomed as an international issue. Two early twentieth-century treatises, both available in digital form, document often intense nationality-related diplomatic episodes and pronouncements: Edwin Borchard's *The Diplomatic Protection of Citizens Abroad* (Banks 1915) and volume 6 of John Bassett Moore's *Digest of International Law* (Government Printing Office 1906). John D. Rockefeller Jr. commissioned a blue-ribbon study of the issue in the lead-up to the 1930 Hague Codification Conference. The group, hosted by Harvard Law School and including two future World Court judges, published its report and recommendations in volume 23 of the *American Journal of International Law*. A good mid-century overview of the subject from a legal perspective can be found in Paul Weis, *Nationality and Statelessness in International Law* (Hyperion 1956).

Chapter 1

On the history of citizenship in an Anglo-American context, see James Kettner's splendid monograph *The Development of American Citizenship, 1608–1870* (University of North Carolina Press 1978). On Lord Coke's famous decision setting out the common law rule of birthright citizenship, see Polly J. Price, "Natural Law and Birthright Citizenship in Calvin's Case (1608)," 9 *Yale Journal of Law & the Humanities* 73 (1997). On the citizenship status of pre–Civil War blacks in the United States, see Martha S. Jones's recent *Birthright Citizens: A History of Race and Rights in Antebellum America* (Cambridge University Press 2019). For an intriguing take on the *Dred Scott* decision, see Randall Kennedy's "Dred Scott and African American Citizenship," in *Diversity and Citizenship: Rediscovering American Nationhood* (edited by Gary Jacobsohn and Susan Dunn, Rowman and Littlefied 1996). Legal

scholar Peter Schuck and political scientist Rogers Smith published
a controversial book, *Citizenship Without Consent: Illegal Aliens in
the American Polity* (Yale University Press 1985), just as birthright
citizenship became a political target, arguing that absolute territorial
birthright citizenship is not constitutionally mandated. That position
has been rebutted by a number of scholars, including most recently
Garrett Epps, "The Citizenship Clause: A Legislative History," 60
American University Law Review 331 (2010). Epps has also addressed the
issue in several articles in *The Atlantic*. President Trump's recent barbs
aimed at the US practice will no doubt generate further commentaries
on both sides. For an interesting historical treatment, including a call
for all countries of the world to adopt territorial-based citizenship,
see James Brown Scott, *Observations on Nationality* (Oxford University
Press 1931).

Citizenship by descent has attracted less critical attention. For
an interesting collection of essays on the topic, see "Bloodlines and
Belonging: Time to Abandon Ius Sanguinis?," available as a working
paper on the EUI website. For a fascinating history of how ostensibly
race-neutral *jus sanguinis* rules worked to exclude persons of Asian
descent from American citizenship, see Kristin Collins, "Illegitimate
Borders: Jus Sanguinis Citizenship and the Legal Construction of
Family, Race, and Nation," 123 *Yale Law Journal* 2134 (2014). The
difficulties of documenting entitlement to birthright citizenship
are explored in *Citizenship in Question: Evidentiary Birthright and
Statelessness* (edited by Benjamin N. Lawrance and Jacqueline Stevens,
Duke University Press 2017).

Chapter 2
There is an extensive literature on naturalization. Among books on
US citizenship with a focus on naturalization are Hiroshi Motomura,
*Americans in Waiting: The Lost Story of Immigration and Citizenship in
the United States* (Oxford University Press 2007); and Noah Pickus,
True Faith and Allegiance: Immigration and American Civic Nationalism
(Princeton University Press 2005). Gerald Neuman unpacks the
normative aspects of naturalization in "Justifying U.S. Naturalization
Policies," 35 *Virginia Journal of International Law* 237 (1994). On the
racial history of US naturalization laws, see Ian Haney López, *White by
Law: The Legal Construction of Race* (New York University Press 1996).
Sociologist Irene Bloemraad takes a comparative approach in *Becoming
a Citizen: Incorporating Immigrants and Refugees in the United States and*

Canada (University of California Press 2006), as does political scientist Ruth Rubio-Marín in *Immigration as a Democratic Challenge: Citizenship and Inclusion in the United States and Germany* (Cambridge University Press 2000). Liav Orgad considers naturalization tests in *The Cultural Defense of Nations: A Liberal Theory of Minority Rights* (Oxford University Press 2017).

For a fascinating and highly readable account of the rise of investor citizenship, see Atossa Araxia Abrahamian, *The Cosmopolites* (Columbia Global Reports 2015). Ayelet Shachar attacks fast-track citizenship for athletes and other skilled elites in "Picking Winners: Olympic Citizenship and the Global Race for Talent," 120 *Yale Law Journal* 2088 (2011). Shachar and Bauböck edited an excellent collection of essays on the subject of investor citizenship, *Should Citizenship Be for Sale?* (EUI / Robert Schuman Center 2014).

Chapter 3

On the distinctive rights and responsibilities that attach to citizenship, see my "The (Dwindling) Rights and Obligations of Citizenship," 21 *William & Mary Bill of Rights Journal* 899 (2013). On the anomalous status of territorial citizens, including those resident in Puerto Rico, see *Foreign in a Domestic Sense: Puerto Rico, American Expansion, and the Constitution* (edited by Christina Duffy Barnett, Duke University Press 2001). On historical participation of noncitizens in US politics, including voting, see Jamin Raskin, "Legal Aliens, Local Citizens: The Historical, Constitutional, and Theoretical Meanings of Alien Suffrage," 141 *University of Pennsylvania Law Review* 1391 (1993). Making the case for noncitizen voting is Ron Hayduk, *Democracy for All: Restoring Immigrant Voting Rights in the United States* (Routledge 2006). For a study of why democracies worldwide are allowing noncitizen voting, see David C. Earnest, *Old Nations, New Voters: Nationalism, Transnationalism, and Democracy in the Era of Global Migration* (SUNY Press 2008).

On the increasingly common practice of external voting, see Rainer Bauböck, "Stakeholder Citizenship and Transnational Political Participation: A Normative Evaluation of External Voting," 75 *Fordham Law Review* 2393 (2006); and Michael Collyer, "A Geography of Extra-Territorial Citizenship: Explanations of External Citizenship," 2 *Migration Studies* 55 (2014). On the tax obligation of US citizens overseas (and why it might violate international norms), see my "Citizenship Overreach," 38 *Michigan Journal of International Law* 167 (2017); and

Ruth Mason, "Citizenship Taxation," 89 *Southern California Law Review* 169 (2015). For a study of the activity of the more than fifty consulates that Mexico maintains in the United States, see Alexandra Délano Alonso's *From Here to There: Diaspora Policies, Integration, and Social Rights Beyond Borders* (Oxford University Press 2018).

Chapter 4

My book *At Home in Two Countries: The Past and Future of Dual Citizenship* (New York University Press 2016) considers dual citizenship from historical, constitutional, and empirical angles. For an interesting perspective on the opprobrium that once attached to the status and efforts to suppress dual nationality, see Nissim Bar-Yaacov's *Dual Nationality* (Praeger/London Institute of World Affairs 1961). A number of edited volumes have addressed various aspects of the subject, including *Dual Nationality, Social Rights and Federal Citizenship in the U.S. and Europe: The Reinvention of Citizenship* (edited by Randall Hansen and Patrick Weil, Berghahn Books 2002); *Rights and Duties of Dual Nationals: Evolution and Prospects* (edited by Kay Hailbronner and David A. Martin, Brill 2003); and *Dual Citizenship in Global Perspective: From Unitary to Multiple Citizenship* (edited by Thomas Faist and Peter Kivisto, Palgrave Macmillan 2007). A 2018 special issue of the *Journal of Ethnic and Migration Studies*, "Strategic Citizenship: Negotiating Membership in the Age of Dual Nationality" (edited by Yossi Harpaz and Pablo Mateos), considers the subject in sociological and political-theoretic frames.

David Cook-Martín's very interesting *The Scramble for Citizens: Dual Nationality and State Competition for Immigrants* (Stanford University Press 2013) looks at how dual citizenship privileged those Argentines who had access to Italian and Spanish citizenship during the financial crisis there in the early 2000s. David FitzGerald has done pathbreaking work on the Mexican diaspora in the United States, citizenship aspects included; see his *A Nation of Emigrants: How Mexico Manages Its Migration* (University of California Press 2008). For a collection of articles on legal relations in diasporas, including citizenship, see volume 81, number 1 of the *NYU Law Review*, with articles by legal scholars on the construction of citizenship in diaspora. For an argument against dual citizenship, see Stanley Renshon, *The 50% American: Immigration and National Identity in an Age of Terror* (Georgetown University Press 2005).

Chapter 5

Patrick Weil's *The Sovereign Citizen: Denaturalization and the Origins of the American Republic* (University of Pennsylvania Press 2012) recounts the history of citizenship stripping in the United States, including newly uncovered archival material relating to the Supreme Court's constitutional curtailment of the expatriation power. Candice Lewis Bredbenner, *A Nationality of Her Own: Women, Marriage, and the Law of Citizenship* (University of California Press 1999) describes how US expatriated women who married noncitizen men. Recent articles address moves by several countries to revive citizenship stripping in the counterterrorism context, including Patti Tamara Lenard, "Democratic Citizenship and Denationalization," 112 *American Political Science Review* 99 (2018); and my "Expatriating Terrorists," 82 *Fordham Law Review* 2169 (2014). See also Matthew J. Gibney, "Should Citizenship Be Conditional: The Ethics of Denationalization," 75 *Journal of Politics* 646 (2013); and Rainer Bauböck and Vesco Paskalev, "Cutting Genuine Links: A Normative Analysis of Citizenship Deprivation," 30 *Georgetown Immigration Law Journal* 47 (2015).

On statelessness, Laura van Waas's *Nationality Matters: Statelessness Under International Law* (Intersentia 2008) supplies a definitive recent treatment. A strong collection of essays on the subject can be found in *Nationality and Statelessness under International Law* (edited by Alice Edwards and Laura van Waas, Cambridge University Press 2016).

Chapter 6

There is a rich literature on citizenship theory. Much of the work is "liberal nationalist" in orientation, affirming the normative resiliency of citizenship as a location of solidarities and robust redistributionist capacities, for which Michael Walzer's *Spheres of Justice* (Basic Books 1984) supplies the touchstone. David Miller's *On Nationality* (Oxford University Press 1997) is a strong restatement that leaves little room for competitor memberships. Rainer Bauböck's *Transnational Citizenship: Membership and Rights in International Migration* (Elgar 1994) and his other discerning work, including "Toward a Political Theory of Migrant Transnationalism," 37 *International Migration Review* 700 (2003), attempt to bolster citizenship's perimeter in the face of increasing global mobility. Ayelet Shachar explores citizenship's exclusionary implications in *The Birthright Lottery: Citizenship and Global Inequality* (Harvard University Press 2009). Linda Bosniak elegantly situates citizenship in a global frame in *The Citizen and the*

Alien: Dilemmas of Contemporary Membership (Princeton University Press 2006). Christian Joppke delivers an excellent, balanced survey of recent theoretical work in *Citizenship and Immigration* (Polity 2010). His article, "The Instrumental Turn of Citizenship," 45 *Journal of Ethnic and Migration Studies* 858 (2019), updates his thesis that citizenship is inevitably being "lightened." For a hard-edged takedown of citizenship's normativity, presenting a head-on challenge to the liberal nationalists and others who have romanticized citizenship, see Dimitry Kochenov's *Citizenship* (MIT Press 2019).

Yishai Blank comparatively considers local, national, and global citizenship in "Spheres of Citizenship," 8 *Theoretical Inquiries in Law* 411 (2007). Kochenov is a leading scholarly voice on European Union citizenship, for example, "EU Citizenship Without Duties," 20 *European Law Journal* 482 (2014). On the membership elements of indigenous communities in settler states, see Kirsty Gover, *Tribal Constitutionalism: States, Tribes, and the Governance of Membership* (Oxford University Press 2011). On local citizenship, Peter Markowitz's "Undocumented No More: The Power of State Citizenship," 67 *Stanford Law Review* 869 (2015) highlights proposed New York legislation under which state and national citizenship would be decoupled. "Formalizing Local Citizenship," 37 *Fordham Urban Law Journal* 559 (2010), sets out my thinking on the subject at greater length than is possible here. Richard Falk and Andrew Strauss call for world government in "Toward Global Parliament," *Foreign Affairs* (January–February 2001). Global citizenship as such has prompted surprisingly little systematic analysis given its entry into the everyday lexicon, evidence of its nascent state.

INDEX